GETTING IN

☐ ☐ ☐ ■ ☐

Inside the College Admissions Process

BILL PAUL

1) order common aps!
2. gets UT/pm acts

PERSEUS BOOKS

Reading, Massachusetts

Library of Congress Cataloging-in-Publication Data

Paul, William Henry, 1948–
    Getting in : inside the college admissions process / Bill Paul.
        p.   cm.
    Includes bibliographical references and index.
    ISBN 0-201-15491-9
    1. Universities and colleges—Admission.   I. Title.
  LB2351.P33   1995
  378.1′056—dc20   95-18675
                                                           CIP

Jacket design by Suzanne Heiser
Text design by Helene Wald Berinsky
Set in 11-point Janson by Pagesetters, Inc., Brattleboro, VT

2 3 4 5 6 7 8 9   02010099
First printing, August 1995

Perseus Books is a member of the Perseus Books Group.

The sorting out of individuals according to ability is very nearly the most delicate and difficult process our society has to face.

—From *Excellence* by John W. Gardner

 □ □ □ ▮ □

My high school guidance counselor told me that to get into Princeton you have to be a flute player from Missouri.

—An applicant to Princeton

 □ □ □ ▮ □

Elsewhere in the application materials, I have suggested that . . . you should just be yourself. . . . I confess that every time I offer that advice, I remember the comment Mark Twain made: *"Telling a person to be himself is the worst advice you can give to some people!"* Still, that's my advice.

—From "A Letter to Prospective Applicants" from Fred A. Hargadon, Dean of Admission, Princeton University

AUTHOR'S NOTE

To protect the identities of the students and some of the characters whose stories are recounted in this book, their names and other distinguishing personal characteristics have been changed. All the home towns given are fictional. For narrative effect, events that actually took place over several years have been compressed into one year, and the order in which some of the events occurred has been changed.

FOREWORD

Today's high school students are battling ever-increasing odds as applications to America's top-tier schools surge. In the last two years, applications to Harvard have rocketed nearly forty percent. In the last four years, applications to the University of Pennsylvania have soared fifty-four percent. Applications to Notre Dame are up thirty percent in two years, while at Smith College, applications are up fifty-three percent in four years and the acceptance rate has fallen accordingly. Statistically speaking, applicants to Princeton now have about a fourteen percent chance, to Harvard about a twelve percent chance.

These numbers are particularly scary when one considers that over the last few years the number of American college-age students has been relatively low. They belong to what has been called the baby bust generation, which is about to be replaced by another baby boom era, as the children of the original post–World War II baby boomers make their way through school. These "echo" boomers, as they're called, are already swelling America's elementary school classrooms to the breaking point. By the time these students are ready for college, they may have only about a five percent statistical chance of being accepted by America's premier institutions. Applicants to other, only slightly less selective colleges may have but a ten percent or so statistical chance of getting in.

Still, it isn't just the sheer number of college-age students that is feeding the crisis. Ironically, the gates to America's top institutions are closing precisely because they were thrown wide open a couple of decades ago.

On the heels of the 1960s civil rights movement, America's most selective universities finally shed their age-old discriminatory admission practices and began accepting, in steadily increasing numbers, women, African-Americans, Hispanic-Americans, Asian-Americans, and rural Americans. Today, with elite campuses looking more like America than they ever have, college-bound young people are experiencing a surge in expectations, fueled in part by top colleges' efforts to recruit ever more diverse student bodies, as well as by magazine "rankings" that have put the names of the elite universities on every student's lips. In 1994, Princeton, for example, received applications from some 5,100 high schools, compared with just 4,666 in 1991. And with the world becoming a "global village," top-college administrators believe that if their institutions are to continue turning out societal leaders, their campuses must become global melting pots. Elite universities receive applications from more than a hundred foreign countries, as well as from all fifty states. With colleges starting to offer electronic filing, the elite schools will soon seem even less remote to students. Reed College's admissions head, Bob Mansueto, says the advent of electronic filing has the potential, by itself, to double the average number of college applications filed per student.

The increase in the number of students clamoring to get into top-tier universities is also the result of a significant increase in the number of high school students taking a "core curriculum," the minimum generally needed to be considered for admission to a top-tier university. In 1982, only about two percent of American high school students took four years of English, three each of social studies, science, and math, two of a foreign language, and a half-year of computer science. By 1990, about seventeen percent did, thus adding thousands of hopefuls to the applicant pools of selective colleges.

Adding to this rapidly building number crunch is the fact that so many bright students now believe that it's "Ivy or else," as *The New York Times* reported in March 1995. The *Times* explained that "getting into an increasingly rarefied list of the nation's most prestigious colleges, once a status symbol, is now perceived as a survival issue by families who see a future dogged by diminished opportunities, a stagnant economy and heightened global competition."

According to Penn's dean of admissions, Lee Stetson, what's happening in college admissions today is an echo of what happens on Wall Street during tough economic times— a "flight to quality." Many parents believe that a gilt-edged sheepskin is their child's best chance for future success. And even with college tuition up to almost $30,000 a year, buying anything less than the very best might not make economic sense.

What can you, your child, or your grandchild do to get

into a top college? Everyone has an idea about what it takes to get in. Unfortunately, most of those ideas come up short.

For example, if you think that being a high school valedictorian is enough, think again. Every year, Harvard, Princeton, Yale, Penn, and other top institutions turn down hundreds and hundreds of high school valedictorians.

How about racking up great SAT scores? Sorry. The top schools regularly reject applicants who have scored about 700 (out of a possible 800) on these standardized tests. Moreover, with SAT scores about to go up thanks to a recalibration of the scoring system, great SAT scores will soon probably count less than they do now.

How about being a great athlete? A great musician? Yes, top colleges want and need students with these skills and talents. But they always have more gifted applicants than they can admit.

Being student body president may help. But again, applicant pools are always loaded with presidents.

Being able to pay full tuition will help at a number of selective schools, but at the very top ones, admission is "need-blind."

How about sending in multiple applications—say, to twenty different colleges? Perhaps. But if the applicant makes the same mistakes on all twenty, that approach is not likely to help.

Spending big bucks on a private school, or paying thumping big property taxes to support enrollment at an affluent public high school, definitely helps. But even schools of privilege are witnessing a cutback in the number of their students admitted to the most selective colleges and universities.

No matter how smart, talented, or accomplished you, your child or grandchild may be, getting into America's finest institutions this year—or in the increasingly rigorous years to come—requires understanding how this complex, ambiguous, emotional, unfair—in short, this totally *human* admissions process actually works. To do that, one needs to live it, to spend, as this book does, a year with a highly respected veteran dean of admissions at a premier university, with several highly accomplished high school honor students, a high school guidance counselor with an exceptional record for getting students into top colleges, and with others who have, as they say, been there, done that.

This book won't give you all the answers. But it will offer insights that should improve a student's chances of getting into the best college possible, *whether or not* that school is elite. Some of these insights may surprise you, even anger you, as you realize—ideally before it's too late—that you, with the misguided help of your school, may have been approaching things all wrong up to now.

CHAPTER □ 1

It is half past eight on a crisp April morning at one of the best high schools in the United States. Carpooling mothers in expensive station wagons pull into the half-circle driveway and let their kids off at the school's front door. Senior students park their own cars around back in a lot that overlooks a lush green football field with its new all-weather running track.

For the guidance counselors who work at this upper-middle-class high school, this is going to be the best and the worst day of the year. Today many of the seniors will at last find out whether they have been admitted to the highly selective colleges and universities to which they applied last fall.

The students at this particular school have had every advantage—they have taken rigorous courses and pursued a wide range of extracurricular activities to develop their talents; they have sophisticated parents, teachers, and counselors. But the rite of spring they are undergoing today is by no means limited to bastions of privilege. All across America, in farming communities, small towns, center cities, and suburbs on the wrong side of the tracks, bright kids have banked their futures on the judgment of an admissions committee on some faraway college campus.

Some of these highly motivated students are wizards in science and math. Others are actors or musicians or athletes—or all of the above. Some work three jobs to help their families, or have started their own businesses, or have won national championships in rodeo events or surfing competitions. Invariably they have done well in their courses. They are the kind of students their teachers will remember.

Some kids in the admissions pool for selective colleges were pushed into applying by their ambitious parents. Others came to the idea on their own, perhaps encouraged by a perceptive teacher or counselor who recognized their talent and drive. One way or another, these young people have spent years focused on the belief that life will be demonstrably better if they can only get through one big challenge— gaining acceptance to an elite university.

For some of these students, acceptance means simply measuring up to parental expectations and long family traditions. For others, it means gaining access to worlds their parents may not even be able to imagine, worlds of learning and travel and professional accomplishment of the highest order.

But on this special day in April when the admissions envelopes show up in mailboxes—thick ones filled with congratulations, registration materials, and further information; thin ones offering little more than condolences—the butterflies in the stomach are universal.

At our affluent high school, the large guidance room is inundated with kids. Some whisper low in small groups. Others sit by themselves, their body language a "Do Not

Disturb" sign. Over in one corner a girl named Sue is rocking back and forth, crying uncontrollably. Three of her classmates are patting her on the back and telling her it will be all right. So is the guidance counselor and even her younger sister, who has been pulled out of class to lend moral support. You are a great kid, they all say. Keep your chin up. The counselor, Mildred Hayes, a heavyset woman with dark hair, suggests that Sue call her parents. Over the phone, Mom and Dad do their best to convince their daughter that it is not the end of the world. But when the conversation ends, Sue's tears don't.

Sue's day began so differently, so full of promise. Like many of her classmates, she had told the post office to hold her family's mail so she could pick it up in person before school started. She was certain she was going to get a letter of acceptance from the Ivy League university that she had dreamed of attending since she was a little girl. Speaking out of earshot, Hayes tells me that Sue is going through something very much like a death in the family. "She will need time to mourn," she says without irony.

Another girl, Georgette, has also been to the post office. She walks into the guidance room in a short, tight-fitting dress, her head hanging down. Georgette asks a secretary to get her counselor, Millicent Dandridge, out of a meeting. As Georgette waits, she refuses to make eye contact with any of the kids in the room. She is struggling to hold back tears. Dandridge, a thin blonde, hurriedly walks in. Georgette asks if they might go outside for a walk. But it's cold outside! Dandridge seems to say to herself. Then she looks into Georgette's rapidly reddening eyes and quietly says, "Let's go."

As soon as they are alone on the walkway outside, Georgette bursts into tears. Dandridge wraps her arms around her. Georgette sobs that she has been rejected by her top two choices. Dandridge takes her by the hand, and they start to walk slowly. After a few minutes, Georgette regains her composure. Maybe, she says, I'll take next year off and apply again. Dandridge says nothing. She has taken enough walks on early April days to know that this common first reaction is almost never acted upon. After another few minutes, Georgette moans, "I just can't go back inside." Seeing that the girl is in no shape to deal with her peers' prying questions, even the well-intentioned ones, Dandridge tells Georgette to go home.

▢ ▢ ▢ ▮ ▢

Are these kids overreacting a bit, the same way they might, perhaps, at the collapse of their first adolescent love affair? Is this some kind of teen obsession? After all, the ozone layer is thinning, the national debt is into the trillions, and children all over the world go to bed hungry. Can it possibly matter all this much where a bright and healthy young person gets accepted to college? It certainly does to them.

Chilled to the bone, Millicent Dandridge returns to the guidance room to find a dozen seniors milling around her desk, asking one another, Did you hear yet? Did you get in? She spots one of her charges, a girl named Barbara. Barbara has long dark bangs that nearly cover her eyes, but her mouth is clearly visible, and the smile she is wearing tells Dandridge there is finally some good news. Where did you get in? the counselor wants to shout, but she knows the girl is shy and that a lot of kids are nursing open wounds. So Dandridge and Barbara go off to one side, and Barbara happily says she got into one Ivy school and onto the wait list at another. This time there is a joyous embrace. Barbara disappears into the crowd, and Dandridge walks over to Mildred Hayes, who has been observing this outpouring of human emotion. Dandridge tells Hayes about Barbara, adding that the university that put Barbara on its wait list rejected another of her counselees who had a higher rank in class.

"So what else is new?" Hayes says.

Dandridge and Hayes talk about Robert, a student who has heard from most of the colleges he applied to but has yet to get into one of them. "I am very, very worried about Robert," Hayes says. "I think he applied very unwisely. I sat down and talked with him about it. I talked with his mother and father about it. The parents said their son is much better than anybody gives him credit for and that these are the schools they're going with. Period." The schools he applied to were Harvard, Princeton, and Pennsylvania. "The boy is smart. Make no mistake about that," Hayes says. "He's in the top ten percent of the class, but he doesn't stand out. He isn't a star."

Another girl, this one named Tish, interrupts to ask the still-chilled Dandridge to go outside for a walk. Here we go again! the counselor says to herself. Outside, Tish pulls her long blond hair together in one hand to keep it from flying around in the wind. In front of the school, she tells Dandridge that her mother has forbidden her to speak to anyone about which colleges did and did not accept her. Tish says that because she has been rejected by her top choices, her mother is furious at everyone, including Dandridge.

"Are *you* furious at me?" Dandridge asks.

"No," Tish says, then sheepishly adds that, because of her mom's admonition, she still doesn't want to be seen talking to her.

Back inside, a girl named Robin bursts into the guidance room. Robin already stands over six feet tall, but her long thin legs suggest she still has a few inches to grow. Smiling from ear to ear, she tells the two counselors that she has been admitted by an Ivy school whose name is known in every corner of the world. "Can you believe it?" she says dreamily. "Call the coach!" barks Hayes. The coach? Hayes says Robin was recruited to the Ivy school by the basketball coach, who told her to call him if the news was good. As soon as Robin leaves, so does Hayes's happy look. When I ask what's wrong, Hayes says, "I like Robin. But there were other kids who were better academically than her who didn't get in."

Out of breath, a happy girl named Amanda rushes up to the counselors. Amanda had waited for the postman to deliver the mail to her home, and when he didn't come and didn't come, she went out looking for him on foot. After running him to the ground and getting him to dig to the bottom of his bag, she had ripped open a letter of acceptance to a fine university, though one less choosy than most of the Ivies. "I've died and gone to heaven!" Amanda says, then rushes off again. Meanwhile, Sue, still mourning, stares blankly out a window with a friend holding her hand.

In strides Rick, the blond and muscular class valedictorian. Wearing jeans and a shirt that shows his bulging neck muscles, Rick is also the school's star athlete and president of the senior class. He applied to four of the five most selective major universities in America: Harvard, Princeton, Yale, and Stanford. (Rice was the fifth in 1994.) When he opened his mail this morning, he found not a single letter of rejection. Word of Rick's success quickly spreads around the room, and a number of curious juniors who have dropped by begin chanting Rick's name and rhythmically pounding on the tables and desks. On this day, Rick has become an instant legend for those who will soon undertake the same perilous passage. And yet Rick's record is not perfect. While none of the four elite universities rejected him, only three actually accepted him. Even though he was the ace of his high school class, Rick was good enough only to get on the wait list at Princeton.

CHAPTER □ 2

It usually begins during the student's junior year. That is the time when high school students and parents start talking seriously about their expectations for college. They sit down with a guidance counselor. They go to College Night, an American ritual where representatives of dozens of colleges and universities visit a high school, hand out literature, and answer questions. Then they buy *U.S. News & World Report*'s latest college survey to size up the test scores and grade-point averages of applicants to America's most selective universities.

Of course, many parents also help their children prepare for the Scholastic Assessment Tests (SATs), which come in the spring. Some drive their children to and from special classes. Some push their children to enter regional and national competitions in science, drama, or debate. Some write letters to college department heads and coaches. Some put together portfolios of their children's art or make audio or videotapes of their children playing the cello or throwing a winning touchdown pass. But given the confusing and seemingly contradictory world of college admissions, shrouded as it is in mystery, no one seems to know how much of this effort is wasted and how much is on the mark.

Back in 1948, Archibald MacIntosh of Haverford College observed that a "cloudy curtain" hangs over college admissions, preventing outsiders from knowing whether the process is a "bad song and dance act, an esoteric nature rite or self-conscious but honest public service."

About one aspect of the process, however, admissions deans of today are clear: most of the applicants they reject have nothing "wrong" with them or their applications. College admissions today is not a head-to-head competition but a process where children are judged against an "ideal" set of academic and personal accomplishments. That fact, however, only deepens the mystery behind who gets in and who does not.

During junior year parents find ways to talk to their children's favorite teachers, preparatory to asking them to write letters of recommendation in the fall. Friends swap "secrets" on how to gain an edge. A woman whose son got into Harvard the previous year finds herself surrounded in the supermarket aisle by parents who want a complete debriefing. The alumnus who interviews applicants on behalf of Yale gets invited to dinner parties by people he hardly knows.

Parents who themselves are graduates of elite institutions volunteer to do alumni interviews, hoping not just to raise their profile but to pick up pointers. For the same reason, those who can do so sometimes make unusually large donations. Some write letters of recommendation for their classmates' kids, even if they haven't seen them since they were tykes, in hope that the favor will be returned. Many start dropping references to and stories about their alma mater into family conversations, so that the child will be able to show familiarity with the school on his application and in his interview.

At a conservative estimate, Americans spend about $250 million a year to gain a competitive edge for their children in college admissions. That figure does not include the huge hidden cost of sending one's child to an elite private secondary school, or paying superhigh property taxes to live in a community that has a top-drawer public high school. Of course, a great many parents of bright kids lack resources to pay these costs. And a great many bright, ambitious kids have parents insufficiently experienced or sophisticated to provide much help at all. Teachers and counselors vary widely in their knowledge of the admissions process and in their ability to guide their students through this maze, even in good schools.

SAT review courses are the biggest slice of a rapidly growing service industry dedicated to giving college-bound students an edge, or at least to compensate for hitherto inadequate preparation. Many bookstores now devote entire sections to college selection, ranging from guidebooks to advice books to practice-test books to "successful" essay books. Summer programs, many of them sponsored by prestigious colleges and universities, give students an impressive-sounding credential to put on their applications, in addition to whatever education goes on there. Independent college counselors go into business to do what high school counselors should be doing but often don't have the time, training, or both, to do. For a fee of up to two thousand dollars or more, an independent counselor will work one-on-one with a student for a year or longer, helping the student pick out colleges to apply to and advising him or her on how to fill out applications, what to say in interviews, and so on. Music teachers and sports camps hone a child's special talents, which also look good on an application.

Some of that money is wasted. Taking an SAT review course can significantly raise an applicant's test scores. But if those test scores aren't supported by grades, teacher recommendations, and so on, a high SAT score won't do him much good and can, in fact, hurt his chances for acceptance. (A university's admissions department will ask: Why didn't the student do equally well in the classroom?) The magazines and guidebooks an anxious parent buys will provide, at best, a superficial look at institutions. If an admissions officer thinks that an applicant's essay has an impersonal and generic style, the expensive independent counselor may be blamed.

Some parents would do better to stay out of it altogether. These are the parents who intervene too much in the process. They ask a university for a breakdown on how many of its undergraduates major in each of its academic departments, then have their child mark on the application that he or she wants to major in a certain underpopulated department, even when the child obviously has no preparation in that subject. Some parents refuse to leave the room during their child's alumni interviews, raising obvious questions about their offspring's maturity and independence. Some call the admissions offices themselves—or worse, have a secretary call—to ask for applications and schedule interviews, prompting a dean of admissions to ask sarcastically: Does the student speak yet?

Then again, sometimes the student applicants themselves go too far. One year an applicant to Wesleyan sent in a scrapbook of his accomplishments that started off with a photograph of his own birth. Another Wesleyan hopeful sent in a six-foot Raggedy Ann doll with a tape recording of the applicant's essay read in a doll's voice. When the admissions staff considered this applicant, one member suggested that the doll be cremated and its ashes sent back to the applicant. Cooler heads prevailed, and the doll was unceremoniously tossed into the garbage.

⬚ ⬚ ⬚ ▮ ⬚

By far one of the most useful of the exploratory rituals takes place during the summer after junior year, when parents hit the road to visit college campuses. Often the parents return to some of them in the fall with the child, so that the child can sit in on classes and meet with a professor in the department he or she is thinking of majoring in. (Professors often jot down their impressions of the kids they see, then send their notes over to the admissions department.) By the start of senior year, parents usually have gotten their children to settle on the colleges they want to apply to and to send away for the actual applications.

Having already observed students at the end of the admissions process, I wanted to talk to some and their parents at the beginning. So, on a steamy summer morning not long ago, I was on the campus of Princeton University with a group of parent and student visitors. Giant raindrops were plopping in twos and threes onto the walkways that crisscross the expansive lawn, and the giant oak trees almost, but not quite, provided a natural umbrella.

Our guide was an undergraduate, a pleasant young man with dark curly hair and small round glasses. His glasses gave him a studious look, despite his oversize white T-shirt, baggy shorts, floppy sneakers, and baseball cap. "Try and keep together," he told us as we started across the lawn in the direction of a long rectangular building with a bell tower, some fifty yards in the distance.

Apart from myself, all twenty-two group members were parents accompanied by their teenage children. One father and son wore matching blue blazers. Another dad looked like he had stepped out of a Calvin Klein ad and his daughter out of *Teen* magazine, while one particular mom seemed outfitted for an African safari. Among those in attendance were Phil Serkin and his daughter, Mary, who had left their Pennsylvania home at the crack of dawn for the one-day trip to New Jersey. The next week they would drive on to Connecticut and Massachusetts. By the time they were finished their trip, they would have seen Princeton, Harvard, Yale, Wesleyan, and Amherst.

Tom Masters, a burly man with sweat beading up on his forehead, had driven up from Florida with his wife and daughter, Debbie. Like the Serkins, the Masterses were visiting several places, including Princeton, Harvard, and MIT, but were cramming them all into a one-week marathon. They had already been on the move for five days, and at this point Tom, obviously worn down by the itinerary, was having a hard time keeping up with the group.

Another family, the Zapatas—father Ray, mother Helen, and daughter Louise—had come from even farther away: Colorado. They also showed the strain of living out of a suitcase for nearly a week. After today, it would be three colleges down and two to go, the remaining two being in education-intense Massachusetts.

The stress and strain on these families was obvious to me. Since this kind of trip was not cheap, I wanted to find out what had motivated these exceedingly conscientious parents.

After the Princeton tour, I caught up with Tom Masters and asked him if he thought all the effort was worth it. "Are you kidding?!" he said, wiping his face with a handkerchief. Masters wore Bermuda shorts and a polo shirt soaked with perspiration. He stood on the sidewalk outside the admissions office, waiting for his daughter's group information session to end. The gnats were biting, and Tom and I slapped ourselves as we talked.

"A degree from an elite university puts you a leg up in your career," he told me. "I've worked at companies where they won't even look at anyone else. Then after you're hired, you've got connections all the way up the corporate ladder. When I tell people that I got my diploma from St. John's University, they say, 'Where's that?' The education you get at an elite university is almost secondary. In real life, it's who you know, not what you know. Always has been, always will be."

A moment later, Phil Serkin joined us. Serkin maintained a cool, stylish appearance in tan slacks and penny loafers. I asked him, too, about the costs and benefits of jumping through all these hoops. "I don't think there's any connection between where you got your education and what you accomplish in life," he said. "Look at me. I'm a doctor. I'm respected in my profession. I didn't go to an Ivy university, and I've done well."

We nodded, traded glances, and slapped at the bugs for another moment. After a bit more thought, Serkin amended his position, admitting that it had taken him longer to establish his medical reputation than his Ivy-degreed partner.

"I have more talent than he does," he said, "but I'm only now getting the recognition." He put his hands into his pockets, then looked me in the eye. "I don't want my daughter to have to go through that. To tell you the truth, I want to make damned sure I give her the headstart I didn't have."

In time Ray Zapata joined the conversation. A short man, he carried a layer of middle-aged flesh over his weightlifter's physique. "I work for an engineering firm," he told me. "I hire five or six people a year. Nearly everyone I've hired recently was a graduate of a very selective university."

I asked him why he always went with the pedigree.

"Why? Because they are smarter, they think more creatively, work harder, and are better organized than other people."

I knew that Ray Zapata would get no argument from most alumni of elite institutions. The life histories of typical graduates of Yale and Harvard support his faith that a degree from a selective college is a sort of "bottled in bond" seal of approval regarding talent and training.

In 1993, on the occasion of its twenty-five-year reunion, the Harvard Class of 1968 took a survey of its several hundred members. More than fifty percent responded, of whom a quarter said they were millionaires. Only one in ten reported having a net worth under $100,000. One-fifth were doctors, another fifth lawyers. Most appeared to be happy and prosperous people.

The Yale Class of 1968 conducted a similar midlife survey. Lawyers and doctors predominated, with educators a clear third. There also were many whose business was money: bankers, investment counselors, and financial service managers.

Only three out of 554 said they were in poor health. A vast majority agreed with the statement: "I am happy with the quality of my life."

Nevertheless, in the last decade, the wave of white-collar layoffs that has swept over corporate America has raised questions about the extent to which a degree from any university can be the ticket to the good life. In his 1985 book, *Choosing Elites*, Robert Klitgaard quite logically suggests that the lifetime success of graduates of elite universities is probably due as much to the personal characteristics that got them *into* those schools as to anything that happens while they are enrolled there.

In 1991 a massive book that distilled twenty years of scientific research on elite graduates went so far as to conclude, in essence, that the importance of a degree from a prestigious university is vastly overrated. The book, *How College Affects Students* by Ernest T. Pascarella, professor of higher education at the University of Illinois at Chicago, and Patrick T. Terenzini, professor and senior scientist at Pennsylvania State University's Center for the Study of Higher Education, analyzed more than 2,600 separate studies conducted during the previous two decades. When it comes to the actual learning that goes on in college, the authors found that "only a small and perhaps trivial part is uniquely due to the quality of the college attended." The same holds true for a young person's "cognitive and intellectual development, other psychosocial changes, the development of principled moral reasoning, and shifts in attitudes and values." It is "individual aptitude differences," the authors concluded, that determine how much students learn in college. According to these authors, then, one can get as good an education from Michigan State as from Brown or Bryn Mawr.

But what about the "long view"? What about life history and earnings? After all, we all know there's more to be gained in college than pure "intellectual development."

Here too Pascarella and Terenzini trim the Ivy down to size. "In the area of earnings," they write, "where the evidence is perhaps the most extensive and the impact the largest, even our most liberal estimate is that less than 2 percent of the differences in earnings is attributable to college quality."

Not that these authors entirely discount the value of attending a highly competitive university. "For example, attending a selective or prestigious college has small positive net impacts on educational aspirations, plans for graduate or professional school, and choice of an academic career, particularly in high-status disciplines, and choice of sex-atypial majors and careers among women. Thus, elite colleges not only recruit ambition, but they tend to nurture it, at least to a modest extent."

But again, the authors conclude that it is individual aptitude, and not the selectiveness or prestige of an institution, that most significantly affects a person's chances for success in later life. "To be sure, there is evidence to suggest that, on average, students attending elite colleges may derive some small advantages in career mobility and earnings. The key words, however, are *may* and *small*. It is unlikely that the net socioeconomic advantages of attending one of the 'best' colleges are anywhere near as certain or pronounced as the public mythology would lead one to believe."

With all due respect to Professors Pascarella and Terenzini, try explaining that to a kid who has always dreamed of going to CalTech, or to parents desperate to give their child the social and economic leg up that schools like Smith and Amherst have always seemed to provide.

In his book *Educating for the 21st Century*, Mark H. Mullin, headmaster at St. Albans School in Washington, D.C., notes that today's "fast track parents are accustomed to keeping score of success, whether that score is measured by financial rewards or powerful positions. In the same way, there is a natural tendency for such people to keep score with their children. The highest points go to those whose children are admitted to the most selective colleges."

Of course, some parents overdo the search for future competitive advantage. Still, there are plenty of reasons to strive for admission that have nothing to do with an external "score card": the sense of validation that comes with winning a place in elite company, the desire for an intense challenge, the invigoration that comes from so much talent concentrated in one place, and the rich traditions of our elite colleges. These, too, are among the reasons that far more families rise to the bait than can ever be accommodated in the venerated halls of ivy. Hence the sleepless nights and the storm and strife—and the $250 million a year to crack the system.

This book attempts to eliminate some of the mystery, to raise the cloudy curtain that shrouds the college admissions process. It attempts to give anxious students, parents, and anyone else interested in the way our institutions assess and reward merit, a detailed play-by-play account of the complex interaction between two seemingly opposing forces. We will follow the progress of five actual honors students (whose names have been changed, of course) and one perhaps-archetypal admissions head, whose identity has not been changed: Fred A. Hargadon of Princeton University. Three of the five students applied to college one year, two another year. Their stories have been interwoven to take the reader through a typical admissions cycle.

How do students prepare themselves for the college admissions process? How do they cope with the pressure? What roles, good and bad, do their parents play? What about high school teachers and counselors? Fundamentally, what is the dean of admissions at a place like Princeton looking for, anyway? How does his mind work?

What value do sports and other activities have in an application portfolio? What about the applicant's ethnic, racial, and geographical background? How about the all-important essay, and the interview? Can a student tailor his or her presentation to fit demand? When do they shoot themselves in the foot, and when do they shine? In short, what works and what doesn't?

Much will be revealed as we follow these intertwined stories, far more than can be gleaned by studying the bare facts in the typical guidebook. While we are focusing on one university's committee, we will compare and contrast the specifics with other schools. What emerges, I hope, will be some useful specific information on the process and the pitfalls, as well as a perspective on how to plan for and think about the meaning of higher education for you, your children, and our supposedly merit-based society at the end of the twentieth century.

CHAPTER ❑ 3

In September about seventy-five alumni who interview candidates on behalf of the Princeton admissions department gathered outside the auditorium of the molecular biology building. Over coffee and bite-sized Dunkin' Donuts the group around the refreshment table was laughing and joking with a tall man with long arms and big hands. He had short gray hair, a deeply furrowed brow, and deep-set eyes— Princeton's legendary dean of admission, Fred Hargadon. As I wedged myself into the middle of the group, two teenage girls arrived, with one of the girls' mothers. While the meeting was for alumni only, Hargadon indicated that he had no problem with their being there. He was concerned only that the speech he was about to give, in which he would emphasize how hard it was to get into Princeton, would frighten them into not applying.

After the coffee and doughnuts, we settled into the auditorium. Hargadon was introduced from the stage by one of his lieutenants. He strode to the platform, a sheaf of papers under his arm, then grasped the podium. He looked us over for a moment, then said in a sharp, no-nonsense voice that he was going to give us "some idea why you don't understand" how the Princeton admissions process works.

As the house lights dimmed, even this group of alums was slightly intimidated. On a large screen at the front of the room, a graphic appeared, showing that 1,534 high school valedictorians had applied for admission to Princeton the previous year. "Now," the dean said, "of that 1,534, how many do you think we offered admission to?"

Hargadon paused.

"About 495," he said. In the audience there were audible gasps. The dean paused again. "How would you like to be one of the eleven hundred who managed to achieve that in high school and then get a letter telling you you're not being offered admission to Princeton?"

Another graphic appeared on the screen. Last year's group of applicants included 2,669 students who had scored between 750 and a perfect 800 on their math SAT. Of those, only 650 had been accepted, roughly twenty-four percent. The dean summarized the situation very succinctly: "A lot of people wonder just what it is we are doing." Then he went on to explain.

☐ ☐ ☐ ❙ ☐

Dean Hargadon's office is located off a large grassy green on the first floor of four-story West College, just behind Nassau Hall, Princeton's historic original building. Built before the Civil War, West College was originally a student dormitory. Sprouts of ivy cling to West College's tan stoneface, remnants of a thick ivy wall that was trimmed back because it was chewing up the facade. The private office of the admissions dean occupies the front left-hand corner of the first floor. As offices of deans of admissions go, this one isn't very flashy. Lee Stetson, Hargadon's counterpart at the University of Pennsylvania, has a posh office that measures about eighteen by twenty-four feet, with reproduction Colonial wing chairs and tables and a large, richly polished wooden desk, plus a large conference table. By contrast, Hargadon's private space measures roughly fifteen feet by eighteen. A squeaky swivel chair sits behind an old gray metallic desk, across from which are two straight-back chairs, plus a gray, coffee-stained couch ready for the Salvation Army. A dusty computer sits on a small round table in the corner.

On one of those crisp and sunny September afternoons that make us all want to go back to school, I sat down across from Dean Hargadon, and it struck me why he looked familiar. "You look a lot like Walter Matthau," I said. He shrugged, half smiling, then said, "Thank you, I guess."

The process that Hargadon went on to describe to me is more or less the same at selective colleges and universities all across America. During the summer and early fall, he said, the schools receive many thousands of requests for applications. These come not just from all fifty states but from upward of one hundred foreign countries. Even so, in September, staffers hit the road to visit their feeder schools and to pitch their institutions to high school students in so-called "outreach" areas, a significant effort to get beyond the established networks and the traditional exclusivity of money and social standing.

In October, the first of the "early" applications arrive. Most selective universities have two admitting periods, an early one in the late fall, and a regular one in the spring. Early acceptances are mailed out the first week of December, so that applying early can eliminate the student's angst of having to wait until April for an answer. But students who want to keep their options open must be careful. Some schools have early *action*, others early *decision*. A student who is accepted under early decision, but not early action, is obligated to attend that school. Penn is early decision, while Harvard is early action, meaning that students don't have to decide until spring. Princeton and Yale had been early action, but both recently switched to early decision.

Every early and regular application that an admissions department receives is treated in much the same way. First, the applicant is given two numerical grades: one for academic achievement, and one for extracurricular achievement. In some cases, personality traits are also graded. Second, the application is read by various staffers, who make written comments and, in most cases, recommend whether to accept or reject. Third, the applicant is discussed during a committee meeting. Then a final vote is taken.

After the admissions department of an elite university has dealt with the early applications, it barely has time to catch its collective breath before the process starts all over again with the regular applicants, a group three or four times larger, whose applications must be in by January 1. During both the early and regular periods, alumni from all over the country interview candidates in their hometowns. On-campus interviews with an actual staffer are becoming increasingly rare because they take up too much time.

The testing organizations forward the students' scores,

high schools send in their official transcripts, teachers and guidance counselors send in their written recommendations, and candidates' families and friends contribute letters of recommendation. With all that paperwork, mistakes are inevitable, but usually they are swiftly corrected. One high school guidance counselor recalls a student who got into a selective institution that seemed well beyond the student's reach. When he inquired, he found out that the institution had mailed the letter of acceptance to the wrong person who, coincidentally, had the same name as someone being admitted. The acceptance stood. In the winter of 1994, on the other hand, Cornell faced a potential lawsuit from a high school senior and her family who were mistakenly sent an early decision acceptance. The university offered apologies but felt that admitting the student would set a peculiar precedent. Forty-three other students were also incorrectly notified.

Every year, elite institutions receive applications from superstar candidates—kids whose accomplishments in or out of the classroom leap off the pages. Hargadon told me about a student who was the top prizewinner of the Westinghouse Science Talent Search; as a junior, the same young man had won the Duracell Young Inventor's Contest for his patented talking measuring cup for the blind. Princeton also enrolled the founder of the first high school chapter of Habitat for Humanity and the first high school student to serve on the international board of advisers to that organization, plus a young woman who had published a children's book about an orphan in medieval France who becomes a stonecutter and brings beauty to the world.

In the same class as the children's book author, Harvard

enrolled a girl who had done postdoctoral-level immunology research at the Food and Drug Administration and a young man who had developed a procedure for testing vision for early signs of dysfunction. Yale enrolled a young woman who had done gene therapy on mammary cells and also founded an adopt-a-grandparent program at a nursing home. Rice got a student who had taught a computer how to speak in two languages. Duke accepted a young man who had created "artificial" red blood cells. Stanford enrolled a young man who had done research on connections between ultraviolet radiation and cancer. Vanderbilt enrolled an older student who had created an alphabet for a tribe in Nigeria.

Other readily apparent superstars each year include the small number of Presidential Scholars, National Science Foundation Young Scholars, and National Endowment for the Humanities Young Scholars.

The genius of other applicants, however, is less visible and must be teased out of the application materials. In October, Hargadon came across a young man whose transcript indicated that, as a junior, he had scored a perfect five on his advanced-placement chemistry test without having taken a single course in chemistry. Was this a mistake? Hargadon wondered. One of the teachers' reports told him it was no mistake: the young man had taught himself chemistry in his spare time.

Fortunately for all the other applicants, there are never more than a handful of superstars each year. Parents and applicants wondering what it takes to get into elite universities might seem well advised to forget about the superstars, because they are just too good, and concentrate instead on being the first in line after them. In fact, that's a mistake, because the superstars represent the clearest models of the type of student an elite university wants. Most students accepted by an elite school will be very like its superstars—only somewhat less luminescent.

The first step in understanding what it takes to get into a prestigious university, Hargadon reminded me, is to understand why having great grades and test scores isn't enough. Virtually every applicant to an elite institution has great grades and test scores. Before the elite universities choose them, America's smartest students have already chosen to apply to these elite schools. This self-selective process accounts for the fact that between eighty and ninety percent of the applicants to a given elite institution are qualified to do the work. (Ironically, anecdotal evidence suggests that the more selective the university, the higher its percentage of qualified applicants.) There is no obvious reason for an elite university *not* to admit most of its applicants. For this reason admissions departments focus on reasons *to* admit students— and those are the reasons that go beyond their grades and test scores.

❑ ❑ ❑ ❙ ❑

Dean Hargadon and I had talked for about an hour, and as we stepped out of his office, our conversation became more casual. He had added a section to the Princeton application, he said, called "hodge-podge," where applicants are asked to give their favorite course, word, time of day, newspaper section, and so on. It was one of his favorite sections, and he often started with it when reading an application. "It's worked out even better than I thought it would. I wanted to relax them," he said, while at the same time subtly testing them. "When you say 'What's your favorite word?', there are a handful of people who really worry that if they name one word it will be the 'wrong' word. And so they say, 'I can't pick one.' I can tell you right now, that's a different kind of person than the person who simply picks Fahrfignugen, or whatever that Volkswagen word is."

I immediately asked him whether this was how he separated the one he admitted from the five or six he did not.

"Well, not always," he said. "But it reveals more than you think. First off, look at my instructions."

The instructions read: "Obviously there are no 'right' or 'wrong' answers to the following questions. We just thought your replies might help us to know you a little better. *Please don't lose any sleep over the answers to this question.*"

"And then," Hargadon went on, "you get one back that says at the bottom: 'Please don't lose any sleep over my answers.'" The dean laughed. "I start liking the kid right away."

Reading applicants' hodge-podge answers, Hargadon said, was as close as he could come to having a conversation with each of them. If he could literally chat with every applicant, he later told a group of alumni, he would be able to pick "the best freshman class ever."

I asked him what *his* favorite course was.

"It's not mine, but I liked the kid who wrote 'golf course.'"

"Well, then, what's your favorite word?"

"If I told you that," he said, "then everyone would put it on their applications."

"Aw, come on."

"It's 'serendipity,' " he said.

"Why?"

"Because my life has been a series of serendipitous events."

Later that fall, Hargadon told me more about himself. His father was a first generation Irish immigrant. Both of his parents had eighth-grade educations. They lived in a small house on a modest street just outside Philadelphia where his father worked on an automobile assembly line.

Hargadon has many vivid memories of his childhood: wiping down the butcher block on Saturdays and putting the money he made from that part-time job into a glass jar his mother kept; sitting on the front porch on summer evenings as his parents chatted with neighbors out for a stroll. But what still chokes him up today is the memory of the morning after his father died when a next-door neighbor got up before sunrise and filled the coal bin in the basement so that his mother would have one less thing to worry about.

While Hargadon's neighborhood was poor, the public schools he attended were not. Hargadon grew up in an ethically and economically mixed community. In these classrooms, rich kids and poor kids sat side by side, but every student was held to the same high standard.

Though he did well in school, Hargadon's parents, teachers, and counselors had no expectation that he would go on to college. He worked, then was drafted into the army. Mustered out two years later, he went back to the part-time job he had held in high school, as a mail sorter for the post office. With the tuition money available to him under the GI Bill of Rights, he took what at the time seemed like a flier on college, enrolling at nearby Haverford College. But he kept his part-time post office job just in case things didn't work out.

Things did work out, however, sending Hargadon's life in an entirely new direction. He took a course in Russian that so fascinated him that he concentrated in Russian studies in graduate school at Harvard and Cornell. He then taught political science at Swarthmore College, and might still be in a classroom today except that one day he was asked to serve as dean in the Swarthmore admissions office. Hargadon so enjoyed coming into contact with a wide variety of young people that, when he was asked to leave teaching and do admissions only, he gladly agreed. He might never have left Swarthmore except that the provost at Stanford asked him to handle admissions there in 1969. He stayed at Stanford for fifteen years, developing a very precise system for analyzing candidates and becoming such a fixture on the Stanford campus that even after he was gone, the last Stanford class he admitted asked him to be the speaker at its Senior Class Day.

He left Stanford, Hargadon said, because he wanted to be "anonymous" again. He had a chance to be a senior executive at the College Board, one of the preeminent educational institutions in the United States. A year after moving into the College Board's offices in a Manhattan skyscraper, he realized that he missed having day-to-day contact with young people. There was only one job he really wanted—admissions dean at Princeton—but at the time it was filled. While he was at Stanford, the school's paper ran an April Fool's issue in which it reported that Hargadon had been offered the Harvard admissions job. Hargadon stated then that he would much prefer to go to Princeton. When the job opened up, he threw his hat into the ring.

Hargadon was chosen because, as one selection committee member recalls, Princeton felt it needed to put a "human face" on its admissions process, and Hargadon's approach made the admissions process personal to the point of intimacy.

Even though Hargadon is known in some quarters as the "dean of deans" of admissions, at times he still can't quite believe that a kid from his neighborhood ended up where he is. One day he went to hear then-U.S. Secretary of State James Baker speak on campus. Baker, a Princeton graduate, was giving an address on U.S. policy toward Russia. Seated in the audience directly in front of Hargadon was Nikita Khrushchev's granddaughter and famed Soviet expert George F. Kennan. Hargadon was so moved by the experience that upon returning to his office, he wrote his brother that he felt as if he had just "touched the hem of history."

Not long after, Hargadon was reading an article by a Princeton sociology professor that compared the French and American middle classes in terms of what "accomplishment" means to each. By the French definition, the article said, an accomplished person is a cultured person, while in America accomplishment means making money and being successful. For Hargadon, it was *Vive la France!* "The person you're going to have to live with the most is yourself. You owe it to yourself to become as interesting as possible," he said.

Although he became an academic, Hargadon was so intent on being himself that he was lucky his grades didn't suffer. "Whenever I had a term paper due, for some reason my interest got really piqued in reading literature and books that had nothing to do with what I was supposed to be working on. Why all of a sudden I had to read a novel in another area, I could never figure out. I'm sure psychologists have a term for it. 'Displacement' or something."

▯ ▯ ▯ ▮ ▯

Three weeks after we met in his office, Hargadon addressed a group of alumni from the Princeton Club of Philadelphia. The meeting was held on the campus of his alma mater, Haverford, in the suburbs outside Philadelphia. After the business crowd had shaken his hand around the open bar, Hargadon stood before them and spoke about himself.

"I go back to the time when you took the College Boards and they didn't tell you your scores," he said. "Only the college and the high school got them. When I first became a dean of admissions at Swarthmore, I called someone and asked 'Could you tell me what my scores were?' " He paused and chuckled. "It was one of those phone calls you wish you'd never made. I used to call my scores low. I now call them modest."

After the laughter subsided, Hargadon continued, "When people ask me, 'Why were your test scores so modest?' I say, 'Well, there were a lot of questions the answers to which I didn't know.' "

More laughter.

"In fact, I'm still haunted every time I go around a bend or up a hill. You know. That question about A comes one way at twenty miles per hour and B comes the other way at thirty miles per hour, when will they pass?"

The room exploded.

At our first meeting I had asked Hargadon who on campus knew him well. He mentioned Princeton's then director of athletics, Robert Myslik. But when I asked Myslik what kind of person Hargadon was, he looked surprised. "I really don't know him all that well," he said.

CHAPTER □ 4

On a Saturday afternoon at the start of her senior year, Lucy Simmons sat in a restaurant booth dabbing French fries into the mound of catsup on her plate and talking about her hopes and fears about getting into the college of her choice.

It was warm and sunny outside, and the traffic whizzed past the hamburger joint. Every booth was occupied, and as the waitress took our order, she said it would probably be a while before we were served.

"So where have you decided to apply to college?" I asked.

"To the best colleges in America," Lucy answered confidently.

"And which might those be?"

"Are you kidding? Harvard, Princeton, and Yale, of course. And also Duke. For my safety school, Penn."

I was surprised. "The University of Pennsylvania a *safety* school?"

"My mom is kind of worried about that, too. But my guidance counselor thinks I shouldn't have any problem with Penn. My mom's thinking of talking to her."

"How do you *know* that Harvard, Princeton, and Yale are the best colleges?"

"Because my teachers, my family, and *U.S. News & World Report* say they are."

Lucy spoke with the hard, nasal accent of southern New Jersey as she held aloft a solitary French fry and pointed it at me. "Look, for years now everyone has been telling me how smart I am. Like in nursery school, I was reading before everybody else. Then in elementary school they wanted me to skip a grade, but my mom didn't want that. I've always been in the highest reading group. I was valedictorian of my class in junior high school. I've got the highest grade-point average in my class going into senior year. The same people who have been telling me I'm smart tell me I should go either to Harvard, Princeton, or Yale because those are the best schools around. And so that's what I want."

Lucy Simmons is exactly five feet tall. She has long brown hair that she keeps in a bun except on dates, deep-set hazel eyes, and thick arching eyebrows. Her bright red lipstick and blue eyeshadow make her eyes look twice as big as they are. At times as she talks, she chews on her fingernails, chipping off bits of red nail polish at the tips.

Lucy lives with her mother in a split-level house in Lewis, a middle-class community, where the cookie-cutter homes have red-brick foundations with wooden frames, nearly all painted white. They have bay windows in the living room, two-car garages under kids' bedrooms, and lawns and shrubs that look like a Miracle-Gro commercial.

Like the house color of choice, the people of Lewis are nearly all white, mostly of Italian or Eastern European extraction. Most moved out of the city to find some elbow room to raise their kids, but for a growing number of them, that job is now over. Today they regularly vote down school budgets that would raise their property taxes, putting them at odds with their neighbors who still have children in school. The street behind Lucy's house is full of youngsters playing roller hockey. Several of the driveways have basketball backboards. Here and there, a shiny black motorcycle can be seen in a garage.

For the most part, the people who live in Lewis work in industrial parks or commute to Philadelphia, where they hold nonmanagerial white-collar jobs. Lucy's mother is a book-keeper for a doctor in town. She makes ends meet with the help of her ex-husband, whom she divorced when Lucy was nine years old.

Lucy's dad never missed a chance to tell the guys in the office how well his daughter was doing in school, but he moved several states away and almost never put in a personal appearance to see her. One of the few times he came around was to see Lucy graduate first in her class from ninth grade.

When Lucy reached high school, she noticed that many of her classmates, even the smartest ones, no longer seemed motivated to study. They wanted to watch TV and hang out, doing just enough work to get by. But for Lucy there was never any question of kicking back. Her childhood curiosity had hardened into an inner drive to work hard no matter what the other kids were doing. Whatever her early proficiency in reading, Lucy was even better at math. She taught herself subtraction as a toddler, and as a second grader she was doing fifth-grade math.

In high school, unsatisfied with what she was learning in class, Lucy talked the head of her school's science department into teaching her privately after school. During her sophomore year, she took extra instruction in biology; during junior year, chemistry. Still not satisfied, she took additional science classes on weekends at a nearby college.

It was impossible to ignore Lucy's talent in mathematics. While she was still a sophomore, she was tutoring seniors in math. As a junior, she took the math SAT and scored 780 out of a possible 800. She won two math-achievement awards, one from a college, the other from a teachers' organization. At the end of her junior year, Lucy was first in her class, just as she had been the year before and the year before that. She was considered the smartest kid to come along in her town for several years. She was the class genius, the student most likely to succeed.

During the summer before her senior year, Lucy received further affirmation of her academic excellence. She was chosen to attend a summer-enrichment program for academically gifted students in her state. The program, to be held at a prestigious state university, would give Lucy a chance to study science for several weeks with a hundred or so other scientifically gifted high school students.

Lucy arrived at the tree-lined college campus in a jubilant mood. Because she had been hand-picked for this program, she felt she must be one of *the* best students around. She believed she stood a very good chance of getting into Princeton, Harvard, and everywhere else she planned to apply.

Then came the first day of the program. The teacher

started talking, and after just a few moments, Lucy looked around wondering if anyone else was feeling totally and helplessly lost, as she was. No one appeared to be. To the others, this was just a review session; to Lucy, it was uncharted territory.

Later in the day, during the laboratory sessions for her organic chemistry and physics classes, Lucy had the same overwhelmed and panicked feeling. She couldn't keep up with the others. She simply didn't know as much as they did.

My god, she thought to herself, they're pure geniuses.

Lucy came home from that summer session in a state of shock. During the remaining weeks of her vacation, she drifted around the house wondering what she should do about college. Her confidence waxed and waned. Was she nuts to think she could get into Princeton? But then again, maybe she could make it. After all, in addition to her 780 on the math SAT, she had scored a 770 on the math level-one achievement test, a 630 on the verbal SAT, a 690 on the English achievement test, and a 620 on the biology achievement test. Even if her high school hadn't prepared her as well as those other kids from the tonier suburbs, it had still produced kids who got into Princeton—two not very long ago.

Lucy took comfort in knowing that the kids who had run rings around her in summer school had done so in science, not math. She also took comfort that her academic record was better than the records of the two students that her high school had recently sent off to Princeton.

They got in, and they weren't geniuses, she said to herself.

Finally, Lucy felt good because she won awards for outstanding Spanish student and social studies student. Her list of extracurricular activities was lengthy, including school newspaper and literary magazine; the science, computer, and Spanish clubs; and the new-student welcoming committee. She had also performed in school musicals and plays.

So in September she plucked up her courage and sent off for the Princeton application. While the "pure geniuses" would be admitted before her, she felt, there would surely be some places left over. Her teachers and guidance counselor believed she would get in and told her so. And anyway, she thought, What have I got to lose?

▫ ▫ ▫ ▮ ▫

Lucy is one of five students whose senior year we are going to follow in this book. All of the students were chosen, in part, because they were applying to Princeton, as well as to other highly selective colleges and universities. They and their parents agreed to talk on the record, provided their real names weren't used. I met a couple of the students thanks to helpful high school guidance counselors. The others I met through teachers I knew, or as a result of gatherings I attended as a member of Princeton University's Alumni Schools Committee (ASC).

In general, I kept up with the students both by interviewing them and trying to make myself an unobtrusive presence in their lives. I'd drop by their homes, take them out for lunch, or call them on the phone. I intentionally kept the relationships informal. After their senior year was over, I conducted follow-up interviews and was able to fill out the details of important events. Mostly I chose these particular students because, at the beginning of the school year, all of them appeared to have a good chance of getting into the college of their choice.

□ □ □ ▌ □

The second student we will follow is a boy named Josh Hastings. He is five feet ten inches tall, razor-thin, with a marine-style haircut, high forehead, and pug nose. He has brown eyes, thin lips, and a cleft chin, and he wears jeans, tie-dyed T-shirts, and sneakers that are falling apart. So much does he dislike shopping that, when his mother threw his Nikes into the trash not long ago, he fished them out. Josh sunburns easily, so outside he wears a New York Giants baseball cap along with his dark blue Giants jacket. He has long, gangly arms and legs, and when he walks, he clip-clops rather like a horse. He is self-assured yet shy, a combination that makes him seem cocky at times, painfully reserved at others. When he speaks, he sounds as if he has a head cold.

Josh told me once that on the day when the acceptance and rejection letters from colleges come in the mail, he will not open them. Instead, he will attach them to a chain and wear the chain around his neck for several days. "I want everyone to see that this monster called applying to college does not control my life," he said.

I met Josh by accident, through a friend of his mother who knew I was an alumni interviewer for Princeton. Alice Hastings gave me a call to discuss the possibility of an interview for Josh, and while the interview never happened, the friendship was struck.

Josh lived with his mother, father, and year-younger sister in Crystal, Connecticut, a two-hundred-year-old village just over the state line from New York. As houses in town go, theirs is the runt of the litter, but this town is definitely several rungs up the social ladder from Lucy's part of New Jersey. The Hastings house is a small, yellow-painted Cape Cod on a tiny side street, where the postage-stamp-size properties are separated by rose bushes and forsythia. A few blocks away joggers and roller-bladers jockey for position going around a mile-long asphalt oval in a pleasant county park. This is the kind of park where gentrified young mothers bring their tykes to play on the swings while they, dressed in tennis whites, serve and volley until lunch. On the Fourth of July, thousands show up to watch a giant fireworks display and to listen to an old-fashioned, Sousa-style band concert.

Crystal is a town where the commuter train stops to let off powerful Madison Avenue ad executives and Lower Manhattan financial lords. These movers and shakers live on the east side of town and look down their noses at west-siders like the Hastingses. The train tracks serve as a dividing line, and on weekends the parking lot on the west side of the train station is transformed into a flea market, where you can buy almost anything you could at the fancy east-side stores at fifty percent off.

Josh's father grew up on the Lower East Side of Manhattan and began bootstrapping his way up in the world by getting accepted into highly competitive Stuyvesant High School. He and his wife believe there is nothing more important than a good education. They were determined to do everything in their power to ensure that Josh got into a very good college, including living in a town like Crystal.

However one may feel about the tenor of the community,

Crystal's public high school undeniably has an excellent academic reputation. The school is a large, rambling, red-brick edifice with spacious athletic fields nearby. To support it and the rest of the local system, many homeowners pay a princely $6,000 or more each year in property taxes, roughly double what they paid a decade ago.

Josh's mother, Alice, teaches sixth grade in a nearby community that is almost as exclusive as Crystal. His father, Bob, is a corporate attorney for an international conglomerate with world headquarters in New York City. Their combined income would be enough to put them on the east side, but by the time Bob finally paid off his own student loans, he had to start saving for his two kids' education.

□ □ □ ▮ □

One day at the end of his seventh-period history class, Josh's teacher handed back a test on the Civil War. Josh sneaked a peek at the letter grade in the upper-right-hand corner, then quickly folded the test paper in half and stuck it into his history book. As he got up to leave, Sheila, a bright girl who sat behind Josh in a couple of his honors and advanced-placement classes, let him have it.

"Another A, Hastings? Or was it an A plus this time?"

Josh frowned.

"Oh, dear," Sheila went on sarcastically. "What was it? An A *minus*?"

"I wish," Josh said.

Sheila was taken aback. "You mean you got a B?"

Josh opened his history book a crack so that only he could see the grade. "A B would have been nice."

"Hold on," she said. "What are you telling me here? That, like, you got a C on a test?"

Josh looked at Sheila morosely and nodded.

"Unbelievable! Wait till people hear about this."

Sheila took off. As Josh made his way out the door, his teacher called out to him, "Hold on a second."

Josh hung his head and waited.

"You and I both know that you got an A on that test," the teacher said. "Why did you lie?"

"Because it's easier. Understand?"

Throughout his school career Josh had struggled with his reputation for being a nerd. His extraordinary ability in mathematics and his fascination with computers did not help the situation. In an effort to fit in socially, Josh kept his hand down in class even when he knew the answer to a question. When someone asked him how he did on a test, he answered that he got a B or C when he really got an A. But except for a B in music in his freshman year, Josh had never gotten lower than an A on any report card. He was first in his class. His grade-point average was higher than 4.0, which was what it would be if he were doing perfectly in every subject. His average was higher because he took only honors and advanced courses, which are weighted more heavily.

□ □ □ ∎ □

Despite this high-powered performance, Josh had not made up his mind about college. All the other bright kids seemed to have set their sights on the rather predictable big-name institutions. But if Josh wasn't that specific in his thinking, he did know what he wanted *in* a college. He wanted a college that had both a strong engineering program and a strong liberal arts program. He wanted to major in engineering but take a lot of humanities courses. Though he was no master musician, he had played for years in his high school marching band, and he was interested in taking more music classes. Ultimately, he didn't want to be around students who were all engineering majors.

At the start of his senior year, Josh focused his attention on three universities with strong engineering programs: MIT, Princeton, and Stanford. MIT, he felt, didn't have the liberal arts program he wanted, so Princeton and Stanford became his co-first choices, with MIT a distant third. While he did apply to other colleges—including, like the other students we are following, a safety school—no other schools but Princeton and Stanford really appealed to him. On autumn evenings, as he worked at the computer in his bedroom, Josh harbored a low-grade anxiety that he might end up having to go somewhere he didn't want to go.

As was the case with Lucy Simmons, Josh's talent was evident from the start. When he was only three years old, he learned on his own how to multiply. When he was six, his mother gave him a calculator so he could satisfy his fascination with knowing the square roots of numbers.

At first "the system" nurtured Josh's talent. When he was in first grade, he was placed in a special enrichment program with the best students in the third grade. The program enabled Josh to visit museums and other centers of learning.

But as Josh developed beyond the other kids his age, he became a problem for his teachers. In his fourth-grade math class he worked on his own from a geometry textbook while the other kids were doing multiplication and division. One day the teacher looked over his shoulder and discovered he was seven chapters beyond where she had thought he was. The school principal suggested to Josh's parents that he attend math class at the local junior high school. Afraid that their physically underdeveloped son would be picked on by the older kids there, Josh's parents declined.

At this point, the public schools had nothing more to offer him in mathematics. The principal, however, had a friend who was a retired college math professor, and he agreed to tutor Josh. At first the tutor worked for free, but when he asked to be paid for his time, Josh's mother had a confrontation. Alice asked the local school board to pay for the tutor, but the board said no. Only after Alice threatened to talk publicly about Josh's situation did the board relent, and then only after Alice agreed not to make waves.

When Josh's tutor retired for good two years later and no other tutor could be found, Alice put Josh in the math class two years ahead of his age group, a pattern that continued for three years. As a ninth grader, Josh took eleventh-grade honors math; as a tenth grader, he took twelfth-grade honors math. At the end of tenth grade, Josh took the advanced-placement calculus test that not many seniors dared to take. He scored a five—perfect score.

Thus did Josh's parents reach yet another crossroads. At the end of Josh's sophomore year, Josh's father recalls, the school "didn't know what else to do with him." With no school official suggesting how Josh could continue to be challenged in math, school administrators seemed to be hoping that Josh would just take the next two years off.

In the spring of Josh's sophomore year, Alice went to see her son's counselor, to discuss what courses he would be taking in junior year. A short, compact woman with dark hair and a penetrating gaze, Alice knew that even though her son was in the honors track, he had already reached the end of the line.

American educators often criticize tracking primarily as being unfair to students in the lower tracks, but Alice's problem with it was the opposite: now that Josh was finishing the most difficult mathematics course his high school had to offer, he had no math course to take in his junior year.

Alice walked down the brightly colored hallway and entered the counselor's office, with its shelves of college guidebooks. The counselor came in and started discussing Josh's courses. After only a few minutes, the counselor smiled and said Josh's schedule was set. Alice's fears were realized: Nothing had been said about math. As she rose and prepared to leave, Alice was already thinking about the stink she was going to make to the school board. Then she spied a brochure on one of the tables. She picked it up and read about a program for gifted math and science students offered by the state university. Alice asked about the program, but the counselor knew only what was in the brochure.

Thus did the school leave it to Josh's parents to keep their son appropriately challenged in math. Alice made the arrangements for him to attend this special program, once again badgering the school board until it agreed to pick up the tab. Twice a week, she took her son to and from his college class, picking him up after his last high school course of the day, then waiting around the campus for nearly an hour before driving him home. Ironically, while Josh got the highest grade in his college class, it wasn't included in his high school grade-point average.

This was just the sort of thing that made Alice distrust the counselor's ability to help get him into an elite university. More than most parents, Alice and Bob intuitively understood the importance of having an excellent college counselor. One night the three of us were sitting around their living room, sipping coffee and eating cookies that must have registered infinity on the calorie meter. Leaning forward and rubbing her hands, Alice said intently, "Somehow, something special has to catch their eye about this kid. Everybody who applies to Princeton has straight A's or almost straight A's. Everybody has good SAT scores, and outside interests."

By this point, Alice and Josh had already met with Edith Warnock, a high school English teacher who, on the side, was a professional college counselor. Warnock took on about twenty clients per year and had a reputation for getting students to write compelling essays—just what Alice felt Josh needed to put him over the top.

At the end of their first session, Warnock had agreed to take Josh under her wing. Alice left, convinced that once again she had found the right solution. But had she known what was going through Warnock's mind at that moment, she might not have felt so secure. As Warnock waved good-bye from the doorway of her house, she was thinking, What a pain in the ass that kid is.

CHAPTER □ 5

Princeton's dean of admission, Fred Hargadon, often gets to his office before anyone else, sometimes before the sun is up.

He likes to arrive at his office before the campus is stirring so he can read as many candidates' folders as possible before getting caught up in a maelstrom of mail, meetings, and phone calls. He opens the heavy wood-and-glass door, passes through the small reception area with its straight-back chairs bearing the Princeton insignia, makes two quick left turns, and proceeds down a short hallway to his office.

If he doesn't have a meeting out of the office that day, Hargadon generally wears corduroy pants and a flannel shirt from the Eddie Bauer catalog.

After he hangs his jacket on a hook behind his door, he picks up his pipe, bangs it several times on the desk, fills it with Captain Black pipe tobacco, and strikes a match. He goes out to the reception area, brews a pot of coffee, and pours it black into a plastic cup, which he takes back into the office, closing the door behind him. Having usually read *The New York Times* over a cup of coffee at home, he might settle down to *The Wall Street Journal*, although the stack of *Journals* on a nearby file cabinet attest to the fact that he usually gets an early start on the day's work.

By the time his secretary arrives, he may have a stack of correspondence ready for her to type up—usually letters to alumni, parents, and others, concerning the admissions process. The dean likes to answer much of his own mail, feeling that it keeps him in touch with the outside world.

His secretary sits down at a desk in a cramped cubbyhole just outside his door, surrounded by file cabinets. Her desk is almost as messy as the dean's. She keeps a tray of chocolate-covered raisins and M&M's for him, plus a large bottle of vitamin C. At the beginning of the year, the staff gets a memo that says: "Don't Get Sick." On a little coffee table next to her desk are folders for filing the dean's correspondence, marked Faculty, Staff, Princeton, Future, and Travel. Once a letter goes into a folder, it generally stays there rather than being shifted to a more permanent file. Hargadon likes having everything at his fingertips. Also, since the admissions department doesn't have a central filing system, retrieving a filed letter can be a pain in the neck. If the dean wants something out of the file of a candidate from California, someone has to go get it from the file cabinets in the basement. For a candidate from Missouri or Kansas, someone has to go up to the second floor.

There are those who say that Hargadon has a split personality: the affable, approachable Fred, and the stern, distant Dean Hargadon. Undergraduates usually see Fred, while Hargadon's staff often gets Dean Hargadon. Roberto Noya, head of admissions at Drew University in Madison, New

Jersey, spent two years on Hargadon's staff. Noya said that while he learned a lot, Hargadon "was difficult to work for." Hargadon says he tells his staff, "We have no hard feelings against each other. If I blast you for having missed a document or misinterpreted one, don't take it personally." By contrast, when a newly arrived freshman tapped on his office window bearing a plate of cookies, Fred warmly helped her into his private office. "They're *his* kids," said one Princeton administrator, on condition his name not be used. "When he's with his kids, he's like Huckleberry Finn."

To become one of Hargadon's kids—that's what each of my five students is after, each in his or her own, very different way.

□ □ □ ▮ □

On a gray, windswept autumn morning, Sirrka Romanski is waiting for the bus. She looks nervously at her watch. It is the first day of her senior year in high school, and the last thing in the world she wants is to be late. After a few anxious moments, the bus finally comes. It takes Sirrka to the high school in her blue-collar community, then keeps on going. This isn't a school bus—it's public transportation. Sirrka doesn't go to her local high school anymore but to a school in a town twenty miles away. This bus will take her to a train station. The train will take her to another bus, which will then take her to her new school.

As she rides the train, Sirrka looks out the window and thinks about the slumber party she had a few nights ago. Her friends tried desperately to talk her out of going to the other school. "How can you think of leaving when you've got everything right here?" one of them asked. "You're popular. You're the smartest kid in the class. Why give all that up to go to a school where nobody knows you?"

Sirrka could have said that her family was planning to move to this new town, which was true, so why shouldn't she get a headstart? But she didn't want to lie to her best friends. She knew that if she had asked her parents, they would have let her complete high school in the town where they lived. Sirrka assured her friends that they wouldn't grow apart, but she didn't try to explain the real reason that she was pulling up roots. The real reason was that she was afraid that, as accomplished as she was at her old high school, she wasn't accomplished enough to get into the kind of college she wanted to attend. She was afraid that being number one at a so-so high school—a school that had last gotten someone admitted to Princeton a few years before—might not be good enough. And so when her father told her about the upcoming move, she decided to spend her senior year as a tuition-paying student at a high school with an academic reputation second to none.

Sirrka Romanski is five foot one, with long, swirling blond hair. She has a wide face, close-set blue eyes, a narrow nose, and a small round mouth.

Shortly after the beginning of the school year, Sirrka and her family moved into a cramped two-bedroom garden apartment about ten to fifteen miles from Princeton. After years of saving, Sirrka's parents—he a chemical engineer, she a paralegal—were going to move into their dream home—as soon as it was built. That wouldn't be for another six months, but they couldn't wait any longer to move their kids out of the old deteriorating neighborhood and into a suburban community where the streets were safe and the schools good. So they sold the small house they had lived in since coming to America from Yugoslavia in the 1970s. The apartment's main area was a combination living room and kitchen, with a large-screen TV in one corner and a giant fish tank in another. There was enough room for only a couch, two chairs, and a coffee table. Since the tiny breakfast table was always piled high with house blueprints, they often ate off their laps.

It took a lot of courage for Sirrka to leave a high school where she was already ranked first in her class. "To a substantial degree," educational reformer Theodore Sizer has written, "we all are what we believe we are. And we believe, more often than not, what the teachers or the test scores or the immediate community tell us."

Indeed, all through elementary, junior high, and senior high school, Sirrka had been tracked, or put in classes with kids of like ability. According to Sizer and other educators, tracking is detrimental to average and below-average students, robbing them of their self-esteem and desire to learn. Logic then suggests that students in the top track have it made. Most American parents believe that is the case. In 1993, James Keefe of the National Association of Secondary School Principals said at NASSP's convention, "Parents with students in gifted-level classes are a special interest group that wants to keep those classes." An NASSP survey had found that ninety-two percent of junior high schools (grades seven through nine) segregated students by ability.

But tracking can also be a trap for the brightest. Surrounded as they are by so much positive reinforcement, they aren't as motivated to seek out greater educational challenges

beyond their immediate community. They also risk compla-
cency. As Hargadon told me, "If I had a 780 [on the] math
[SAT], I would be feeling very good. I wouldn't feel so hot if I
knew there were going to be another five thousand people like
that applying to the same [college] I am."

For these reasons, being the best in one's school or community is often not enough to get into a highly selective
university. Thinking that it will be enough is a trap, one
particularly dangerous for bright, talented youngsters who
attend average high schools or worse—and the vast majority
of them do. Unlike Sirrka, most of them aren't in a position to
switch to a better school in the next town. What are they
supposed to do to improve their chances?

"In New Hampshire," Hargadon added, "some of the
rural kids will have attended a summer honors program some
place, say St. Paul's. Those are good bets. First off, because
they've really done something extra to improve themselves
academically. Taken advantage. Gone beyond their own
school."

Sirrka also had to overcome obstacles from the community
where she grew up. There she had had to listen to neighbors
tell her immigrant parents to go back where they came from.

As a young girl, Sirrka was self-conscious about being
"different" and tried to "fit in" with the other children in her
neighborhood. For her ninth birthday her mother, who had a
very thick accent, was decorating her cake for her party. Sirrka
looked at the name on the cake and begged her mother to
change it. "But that's your name," Mom said, "the name your
father and I gave you." Sirrka was unmoved. She wanted to
make her name sound more American, so that she would fit in
with the other kids.

The cake stayed the same, but as Sirrka got older, she took more notice of the slights her parents had to put up with. They didn't get invited to neighborhood parties. They were considered odd. They had no close friends. As the years passed, fitting in became less and less important to Sirrka. She gravitated toward following the example set by her father, who had pulled up roots in order to make a better life for his family.

▯ ▯ ▯ ▮ ▯

At her new high school, Sirrka's guidance counselor pointed out the problem with her strategy: Her grades at her new high school might not be as good as they were at her old high school. Even as smart as she was, he said, there would most likely be a period of adjustment, during which her grades would suffer. That sort of thing happened all the time to students making the transition from high school to college, he said. If, for whatever reason, Sirrka's grades slipped during the first half of her senior year, she wouldn't have any time to recover because she was applying for early action at Princeton. "If I were Hargadon," the counselor said a bit ominously, "I would want to see her transcript for the first half of her senior year, to find out just how good a student she really is."

Another problem Sirrka had created for herself, the counselor said, was that she didn't yet know her new teachers well enough to have them write personal, anecdote-filled letters of recommendation, the kind that make a candidate come alive to a college admissions committee.

Like an aggressive gymnast or springboard diver, Sirrka chose a strategy with a higher possible yield but with a far greater degree of difficulty. At the Haverford talk, Hargadon had remarked that applying to college "is probably the first moment in the lives of our sons and daughters that's got all the potential for crisis and pain." Being rejected by Princeton might bring just such a crisis for Sirrka.

▯ ▯ ▯ ▮ ▯

At half past ten on the third Thursday in September, early morning classes were ending, and Princeton students poured out of the great lecture halls and narrow seminar rooms. Shouldering their book bags, they walked or biked across the grassy courtyards. Some descended into the bowels of mammoth Firestone Library to read and study, while others ducked back into Gothic-style buildings for their next class, which would start in ten minutes; still others wandered over to the graceful round building that housed the student center, where midmorning snacks were available.

As Sirrka came out into the sunshine, in bluejeans and a tan sweatshirt with PRINCETON across the front in large orange letters, she looked as if she had already joined the freshman class. She hadn't, of course. The university was permitting a handful of high school seniors in the area to take classes on campus because they had already completed the most advanced class in that subject offered by their high school.

Holding her books under her arm, Sirrka looked at the other students, at one point bumping into a girl who was walking in front of her. After the others reached their destinations, Sirrka still just walked and looked around—at the tall oak trees and the buildings, especially the giant chapel that looked like an English cathedral. Finally, she stopped to read the notices on a large wooden bulletin board in the center of the campus.

She whispered to herself, "I just love it here."

Walking about a hundred yards to the far eastern end of the campus, she stopped and looked down at a section of sidewalk where someone had written his name years ago, imagining her name alongside his. Jazz music blared out of an open dorm window. "Next year," she thought, "I want to be in a room just like that, listening to music and studying, then going down to dinner with my roommates. I'd give anything to be here."

Later when she told me how she felt, I looked at her. "But what do you *really* know about Princeton?" I asked.

"I know I'm in love with it. I was talking to my girlfriend the other day. She really wants to go to Yale. She said it was like she had Yale-blue blood in her veins. I knew exactly what she was talking about. I told her it was like somebody had pinned a P over my heart."

"There's one heart in particular you're going to have to win over," I said.

"Who's that?"

"Fred Hargadon. The dean of admission."

CHAPTER 6

Even the smartest kids need help getting into the right college. Lucy Simmons, up against all those "pure geniuses," was going to need help with her application, especially her essay, so that it conveyed the quality of her thinking, her questioning nature, her openness to ideas—in short, her creative intelligence, which is not measured by grades and test scores. Josh Hastings was going to need help bringing his personality alive to show that he wasn't a nerd but could fit into a campus community. Sirrka Romanski was going to need help getting over the hurdle of being unknown to the teachers at her new school.

Upon entering high school, whether a student is likely to graduate first or last four years hence, it's the guidance counselor's job to map out an academic program that challenges that student to perform at the highest level possible so that he or she can maximize his or her opportunities.

Or at least that's the theory. Frank Burtnett, who until 1994 was executive director of the National Association of College Admission Counselors (NACAC) in Alexandria, Virginia, conducted his own survey of colleges that offer a master's degree in counseling, the degree required of school guidance counselors. He asked colleges whether they offered a course that dealt specifically with counseling for college. Of the 125 colleges that responded, he said, only four taught such a course, and only thirty others said they included such instruction in other courses. In a 1993 article for *Education Week* entitled, "Move Counseling Off the Back Burner of Reform," Burtnett wrote:

> Counselors are prepared today with generic skills that may or may not have application with students in an educational environment. Very few counselors are taught learning theory or the relationship of learning to human growth and development. A recent master's degree graduate of a well-known counselor education program told me of taking a graduate course in educational measurement and never once hearing the term "admission test."

In his opinion, Burtnett told me, "what the counselor has become in many schools is the extinguisher waiting for a fire to break out. We can't put that whole burden for all of these community and social world ills on the high school counselor to solve. And that's been the attitude over the last two decades. Let the counselor do it." As counselors have been transformed from "promoters of academic achievement" into fire extinguishers, "it's flat-out hurt kids. They don't have that ally." Academic counseling in public schools has been allowed to languish because "parents haven't kicked enough butt to demand that these services be available."

> In far too many schools and districts, counseling services are categorized as ancillary, adjunct, or auxiliary in nature; meaning "nice but not necessary to many."

As of October 1992, there were 60,000 more students in New York City schools than in the mid-1980s, but there were one hundred fewer guidance counselors. In California, several large school districts, including Sacramento's, eliminated all school counselors because of budget cuts. Counselors in urban and rural communities often are assigned five hundred or more students. "Counseling," says Terry Cowdrey, assistant dean of undergraduate admissions at Vanderbilt, "is one of the most thankless jobs. So little respect, so little money."

In 1992, NACAC conducted a poll of 3,485 high school seniors attending forty-five public and private high schools across the United States. "Who influences you the most in school when it comes to making your education and career plans?" the students were asked.

Only twenty-two percent said their counselor.

While thirty-three percent said their teachers.

And thirty-nine percent said other students and peers.

☐ ☐ ☐ ▮ ☐

It was a bad break for Lucy Simmons.

As a freshman, Lucy was good enough in math to tutor juniors and seniors. She, like Josh, might have gone on to take college-level math courses while she was still in high school— if, perhaps, her mom had known she had to kick some butt. But knowing about such options, and making arrangements for them to happen, should not be the task primarily of parents, who may or may not be aware of opportunities in the area. Where was the guidance counselor at Lucy's high school, the one who had helped get two of Lucy's friends into Princeton?

This counselor was, it happened, an old hand who knew

from experience what top colleges look for. Over the years he had listened to many lectures delivered by deans of admissions of selective universities, on just this subject. Unfortunately, at the start of Lucy's sophomore year, the man died shortly before she was scheduled to meet with him for the first time. His replacement was a woman who had once been a guidance counselor but had most recently been a school system's alcohol and drug counselor.

Lucy missed this opportunity—through no fault of her own.

Sometime in the next couple of months, Hargadon and company will read the applications of Lucy Simmons, Josh Hastings, and Sirrka Romanski. They will see three applicants ranked first in their classes at the end of junior year. They will ask themselves, among other things, how well each candidate made use of the resources available to him or her. As unfair as it may be to Lucy, Princeton might well conclude that Josh and Sirrka made better use than she of similarly available resources.

Still, that does not necessarily mean that Josh and Sirrka will get into Princeton, and Lucy won't. Maybe all three will get in, maybe none of them will. The students Hargadon admits, he says, must be able to do a lot of different things to keep a university community like Princeton going: they must have musical abilities, athletic abilities, political leadership. What, besides smarts, do Lucy, Sirrka, and Josh have to offer? And what will they say on their applications, especially the essay? In the end, Lucy could still turn out to be the far more compelling candidate.

Clearly, though, as their senior year began, Josh was in better shape than either of the other two.

I couldn't help but think things would have been different for all three kids if they had been at different schools. Sirrka wouldn't have needed to seek out a new environment, Lucy wouldn't have been forced to progress at the class's speed instead of her own, and Josh's parents wouldn't have had to push so hard. At Union High School in Union Township, New Jersey, for example, every student has the opportunity to qualify for an accelerated-learning program, called the Seton Hall/Union Scholars Program. To be eligible, a sophomore must score a minimum of 1,000 on the P (for preliminary) SAT or achieve a 4.0 grade-point average. Students who qualify can take college-level courses at nearby Seton Hall University. The courses are taught by high school teachers, but the teacher, syllabus, and examination for each course must be approved by the university. Courses are offered in math, science, foreign languages, English, psychology, and computer science. In part, the program is designed for students who want to save money by getting a headstart on college and earning a degree from Seton Hall in three years. But students in the program don't have to go to Seton Hall. Seton Hall president and chancellor Father Thomas Peterson told a reporter one time, this program "says to the student who is bored by high school, 'We'll give you an opportunity to do more than high school, but you have to show us you can do it.' "

Unfortunately, most schools do not do as good a job of finding programs for their high academic achievers as Union High School.

❑ ❑ ❑ ❙ ❑

Josh was compensating for his school's deficiencies by using a hired college counselor, one of a steadily growing number of independent counselors who have hung out their shingles in recent years as the quality of in-school college counseling has gone down. How good are they? "Some of the best high-school guidance people I know are now independent counselors," Harvard's admissions head told *U.S. News & World Report* in 1990.

But is it fair to have a system where some parents are able to pay for the kind of quality college counseling that should be available to all? After all, their fees are not low. "I used to feel guilty about charging so much, but not anymore. I'm worth it," said one independent counselor I met. In 1993, this counselor (and a former Ivy admissions staffer) charged up to $2,000 per client for her deluxe services, which included helping students pick colleges that would be a good "match" for them, then helping them fashion an application tailored to catch the eye of someone like Hargadon.

This deluxe counselor was not the one Josh's mom hired. The one Alice Hastings hired charged much less, though it was still a strain on the Hastings's budget. Alice took her on because, by this point, she believed it would be money well spent.

□ □ □ **▌** □

Public high school counselors often have more than 250 students to keep track of at once, and the number keeps climbing every year. Some counselors have modern computer systems, private offices, and conference rooms, plus every college handbook, guidebook, and video imaginable, but they don't have the time to get to know every student as an individual. As a result, students who attend even the best public high schools in America often are at a disadvantage compared with students who go to elite private prep schools.

In their book *Preparing for Power—America's Elite Boarding Schools*, sociologists Peter W. Cookson, Jr., and Caroline Hodges Persell point out that college advisers at elite private prep schools are often responsible for only 65 to 140 students each. Thus they have time to thoroughly investigate each and every student and help shape the college applications of each.

According to the authors, prep-school college advisers do copious research, finding out:

- what the student, and his parents, are looking for in a college
- what colleges they are considering
- where their relatives attended college
- whether they need financial aid
- the summer work, travel, volunteer, athletic, student government, club, publications, or debate activities the student has been involved in
- the books the student has read in the last six months, plus any musical, artistic, or theatrical activities
- what sort of independent research the student has done.

A counselor in the best public high schools may have time to do this research for every student, but for a prep-school counselor this is only the first step. Prep-school advisers often ask students to prepare a written autobiography or self-evaluation. They may ask students to describe how they are unique, what they do best, and how particular experiences have affected them. They often explain to students how to arrange college visits and interviews, what might be asked in an interview and ways to respond, even how to dress for an interview.

At one unnamed boarding school mentioned in Cookson and Persell's book, about half the graduating class goes to Harvard, Yale, or Princeton. The college adviser at this school interviews each faculty member about each member of the senior class. Housemasters and coaches write reports about the students they've come to know. Then the adviser interviews each senior individually. Only then does this adviser write his reports to the colleges. "[E]verything positive that could be said about a student is included" in those reports.

Still, there are very good public school counselors who can more than hold her own against them. At New Jersey's Millburn High School, Nancy Siegel is one of them, even though she is responsible for more than two hundred students.

By the time a Millburn student is a senior, Siegel or one of the three other counselors has likely had several, maybe dozens, of friendly chitchats with him or her—the kind of personally revealing conversations Hargadon would love to be able to have with every applicant so that he could pick "the best freshman class ever." Siegel has turned her office into a Hargadonesque front porch.

The Millburn guidance office is a converted school library, bigger than a classroom. There is a large open area with several round tables and secretaries' desks, and a wall of shelves chockablock with college catalogues, SAT literature, and brochures for academic enrichment programs, such as the summer program for gifted high school students at Oxford University in England. Four small, glass-walled private offices encircle the main area, one for each counselor. The setup permits the counselors to go outside and chat informally with one or more students, or to close the door for an in-depth, one-on-one working session.

Spending a day at the Millburn High School guidance office is like having a front seat at a riot. Students clamor for Siegel's attention. While listening to what the kids are saying to one another about teachers, other kids, and what's going on in their own lives, Siegel is carefully filing away each impression for future use.

Pomona College's Bruce Poch paid Siegel perhaps the ultimate compliment when he said that if every high school counselor were as good as she, the for-hire college counselors would be out of business.

At the start of the school year, each senior is asked to write down the name of his "favorite" book, time of day, quotation, and so on—just as applicants to Princeton are asked to do. Just as Hargadon often starts reading an application by looking at what he calls the "hodge-podge" section, Millburn counselors use the hodge-podge, along with all their other impressions, to write reports that show off the "real" student to a college.

In a quiet moment at the end of the day, Siegel was joined by Ellen Brener, a friend and co-worker. They jokingly recalled how they used to try to do things the way they were taught to—in particular, making separate appointments for students and writing down what happened after each session. "My first year here," Brener said, "all I did was write." Then they decided to do it their own way.

To be sure, Siegel and the others are as much social workers as academic allies. But nor are they just fire extinguishers waiting for a fire to put out. By keeping everything loose and free-flowing, Siegel and company effectively integrate social and academic counseling so that, when it comes time for them to tell colleges about their students, they can describe the "real" student to a selective university.

CHAPTER ☐ 7

At most universities, the process of reviewing an application generally takes at least one and often several hours per applicant. Each application is almost always read by two or three different staff members. Then usually one, but sometimes as many as three different committees review it.

Whether the applicant is a superstar or an obvious reject, the same basic procedures are used. These procedures consist of three fundamental steps: a preliminary rating, an intensive reading, and a final committee meeting. The first and second steps often are combined; a "first reader" also rates an applicant on a one-to-five or a one-to-ten scale in several different academic and nonacademic categories. An institution that has both early and regular admissions will hold two big committee meetings, one in late fall, the other in early spring.

"We're the worst sweatshop in the world," says Barry McFarland, senior associate director of admissions at Rice University, which indeed has one of the most elaborate review processes of any highly selective university. Rice's process is worth looking at in detail because it features almost every conceivable aspect of an admissions process.

The first reader of a Rice application rates the applicant on a one-to-five scale, with five the highest, in five different areas: academic performance; degree of difficulty of high school curriculum; school support (mostly teachers' and guidance counselors' letters of recommendation); presentation; and personal qualities. The first reader writes a full-page narrative on the applicant and recommends whether or not to admit. It is not a decision the first reader takes lightly because, should he or she recommend admission, he or she becomes the applicant's designated advocate.

About one out of four applicants to Rice are all but gone after the first reading. Still, before they are actually pronounced rejected, they get a second read from an associate director in the admissions department, who can (though usually doesn't) decide to put them back in the hunt. For those who move on to round two, their applications are read by a second reader, who also rates the applicant and writes a full-page narrative. The second reader's narrative highlights any differences of opinion he has with the first reader's assessment of the candidate. While similar to the first reading, the second reading of an application is fundamentally different in that it is "national" while the first reading is "regional." This means that the second reader reads applications from all parts of the country, whereas the first reader was reading applications from the section of the country for which he has primary responsibility. The purpose of a national read is to eliminate any bias that the first reader may give a candidate because he or she is personally familiar with the candidate's high school.

After the second reading, about one out of every six remaining applicants is shunted aside, leaving more than half the original number of applicants still in the running. While it may seem that two intensive readings should be able to whittle down the pile more than that, the fact that the applicant pool to an elite university is already highly self-selective, means that there are very few obvious rejects at the outset.

The third reading of an application is done by one of the top three members of the admissions department, one of whom is McFarland. After their reading, however, all that happens is that a small number of applicants are designated for the wait list, as opposed to being added to the reject list, for what McFarland forthrightly calls "political" reasons. One "political" reason for holding off on rejection is that the applicant is the son or daughter of a Rice graduate—a legacy. Another such reason is that the candidate is ranked higher in his high school class than an applicant from the same school who looks like a definite admit. In such a case, the higher-ranked student goes on the wait list rather than the reject list, so that the high school doesn't go ballistic.

After the third reading, the applicant is ready for a committee meeting—though not *the* committee meeting. The application is reviewed by both a faculty committee and a student committee. While involving current undergraduates in the process is quite rare in American universities, faculty involvement isn't. Indeed, at Duke, final decisions on engineering school candidates are made by a faculty committee, with the dean of admissions serving ex officio.

The faculty and the student committees read the applications of candidates who have indicated that they plan to major in the faculty members' and students' respective academic departments: engineering; science; humanities and social studies; architecture; and music. These two committees are strictly thumbs-up committees: They can recommend who to admit, but they have no authority to reject.

For rejection, it's back to the admissions department, which is where *the* committee meeting takes place. More than half the original candidates are still in the running by the time the final committee meeting gets under way. Two faculty members, including the head of the faculty committee on admissions, join the top three members of the admissions department. The final meeting is where the designated advocate argues on behalf of his candidate. More than half of the remaining candidates are rejected outright, while another quarter are put on the "high" wait list, meaning that they, not the ones on the "political" wait list, will be called first, should any spots open up. Left standing are approximately 1,100 to 1,200 applicants out of the original pool of 8,000. When the mailman comes, their letters say, "Congratulations."

As complicated as all this sounds, it's actually even more complicated than I have laid it out here. Rice doesn't have merely an early and a regular admissions period: It also has an "interim" admissions period, which falls between early and regular admissions. Thus, the final committee meets not once but three times a year. Every time McFarland turns around, there's another new pile of folders to read, another group of kids about whom decisions must be made.

□ □ □ ❙ □

At Princeton, the preliminary rating is done before the first reader goes into action. Ratings are made in just two categories: academic and nonacademic achievement. A scale of one to five is used, with one the highest. Each year, only about 10 percent of applicants are given an academic one rating.

During another meeting in his office in October, Hargadon takes a sip of coffee, tips back in his chair, and gives me a brief rundown.

"I look at the test scores," he says. "I look at the transcripts, grades, number of honors courses, and so forth, and figure out whether it's an academic 'one,' which is usually somebody who has five or six [test] scores over 700, probably a 4.0 grade-point average, and at least twenty solids."

A solid, the dean explains, is a true academic course, such as history, biology, and English. For even a true academic course to be counted as a solid, however, the candidate's record must reflect that "a number of those" courses were honors courses.

It's easier for an applicant to Princeton to slip from an academic one to a two than it is to slide down a greased pole. An academic two, says Hargadon, is a candidate with a 3.9 grade-point average and twenty solids.

Hold on. Twenty solids? Hasn't Hargadon just said that twenty solids make a candidate an academic one? No, what he said was that an academic one needs *at least* twenty solids. Twenty-two or twenty-three is preferable.

Here, then, is the Princeton candidate's mission impossible: take five or six solid courses a semester during sophomore and junior years, get A's in all or nearly all of them, then back up that virtuoso classroom performance with half a dozen test scores over 700. Anything less, and the candidate will probably be graded no higher than a two, which, while very good, does not separate that candidate from the pack. (About fifty-five percent of applicants are either academic twos or threes.)

One day while he is grading candidates, Hargadon says aloud, "This candidate is first in a class of 338. He has a 4.0. Seventy-one verbal [meaning 710 on his SAT verbal]. Seventy-five math. Seventy-four English [achievement]. Sixty-seven physics. Probably an academic one."

A few folders later, he draws circles around two of the courses listed on the candidate's transcript. The circles mean that the A's in those courses, which are Vocabulary and Computer Programming, won't count. "If," Hargadon says, "that had been Computer Science instead of Computer Programming, the A would have counted as a solid."

Next up is a candidate who, among other academic accomplishments, has scored a 710 on his Latin achievement test. Hargadon's eyes widen. "You're not going to see many like that," he says. Seconds later, the dean is chuckling. The very next folder he opens belongs to a candidate who has scored a 750 on the same test. "How's that for coincidence?" he says.

As for the nonacademic achievement rating, Hargadon says that to get a one, a candidate has to have done something truly exceptional, such as swimming in the Olympics, performing on the violin at Carnegie Hall, or selling a zillion Girl Scout Cookies and speaking to major U.S. corporations about salesmanship. Asked for other kinds of accomplishments that would make a candidate a nonacademic one, he replies, "They hold a patent. That would be a one. They've published a book. That would be a one."

And a two?

"Two tends to be state and regional levels of accomplishments" in areas like music and sports.

Three?

"Three tends to be the norm of the group. Probably captain of a team. Concert mistress of the orchestra. President of the class. Something more common in our group [of applicants] than people would think."

A four, meanwhile, is someone who is "active but not a leader or exceptional," while a five is "little or no achievement." The competition is fierce.

Just a few weeks earlier, while getting another cup of coffee in the reception area, Hargadon was accosted by a short, round man whose daughter was then in her group interview session. "I just want you to know that I have told my daughter that while she is a sure bet at most of the colleges she's applying to, it will be a little tough for her here."

"That's nice," Hargadon said.

"You know, my daughter is editor of her school newspaper. She's also got a letter in fencing. I'm sure she's going to get into a lot of colleges."

"Well," said Hargadon, embarrassed and very aware of the other parents, who were staring at them, "I wouldn't be able to say that. Let me tell you why." But the man wasn't interested in what Hargadon had to say. He kept talking about his daughter until finally Hargadon broke free.

Afterward, the dean said, "We see a lot of newspaper editors in our applicant pool. Eventually we find somebody who we have reason to believe is a really good writer and where it's not just a title. Where he or she has taken a newspaper that had fifty circulation and now it's four hundred."

Before the school year started, a young man from California visited the Princeton campus with his parents and younger sister. The young man had written ahead of time to say that a mutual friend wanted him to say hello to the dean. During the course of their conversation, Hargadon learned that the young man was a junior national champion in luge, the sport where competitors hurtle down an icy track at breakneck speed while lying flat on their back on a sled. The young man had become a champion even though he lived in southern California, a long way from any luge track. He had taken correspondence courses in high school and done very well in them. Recalling that conversation, Hargadon told me, "I can tell you right now, there's only going to be one candidate in this country who has an A record in high school who was the U.S. men's junior national luge champion."

As exceptionally hard as it is to score high in Princeton's preliminary ratings, it must be remembered that they are just that, preliminary. Not until the readers—three of them per applicant—go through everything in the applicant's folder will it be decided whether those high grades and test scores reflect an applicant who is an active learner or an empty slate. Not until the readers sift through the essays and references will the admissions department get a fix on the applicant's equally important personal characteristics.

▯ ▯ ▯ ▮ ▯

Roberto Noya, the head of admissions at Drew University who spent two years on Hargadon's staff at Princeton, says the reader's job is to find "what are the facts and patterns here" and to "express an opinion on what it all means."

I knew before meeting Noya that the second phase of Hargadon's admissions process involved an intensive reading of everything in a candidate's folder by three different staffers, starting with the least experienced and moving up to the most. (To keep things straight, different-stage readers used different-colored ink to make notes.) Judging from a look around the admissions office, the reader's job was not unlike that of a monk in the Middle Ages. Before Gutenberg invented interchangeable type in the fifteenth century, monks sat all day in cramped spaces elaborately copying books. Here readers sat in small offices all day and often into the night, poring over applicants' files and making copious notes on note cards that became part of the candidate's file. With all this solitary reading and writing going on, a Gregorian chant in the background would have been appropriate.

Noya and I went out for lunch to a local restaurant that had sticky red-and-white-checked plastic tablecloths and a big lobster tank in the middle of the floor. When I asked him for an example of an application that is relatively simple to analyze, Noya lit a cigarette and said, "Take the student who is in the top ten percent of his class. The [academic] program's okay but not great, particularly for Princeton. But it's okay. Hard to argue he's just nowhere near prepared. But hard to argue that he's a lot better than a lot of the other candidates. And the teachers are saying things like 'very good' and 'he's a solid performer.' But no superlatives. And the [test] scores tend to be in the range which says 'Hey, you're not going to worry about this.' But neither are you going to say 'Some of the highest scores you've seen in our pool.' " Such a candidate, Noya said, was good but not great—definitely not someone he was going to recommend.

A more difficult case, Noya said, would be "the student where the scores are spectacular and the teachers are saying this kid is brilliant, [but] you've got a transcript that's up and down all over the place. Now you've got to figure out what the hell's going on here. Is this kid bored silly? Does he have psychological problems? If you're brilliant, way beyond your classmates in high school, if you're not in the right high school with the right teachers, you may very well just out of sheer indifference start getting a few poor grades. When it doesn't match, you've got to notify him [Hargadon] on that reader card that you appreciate that he's going to see it."

With an up-and-down candidate like this, Noya basically would pass the buck. He would write on the reader's card something along the lines of how this applicant "has a lot of raw ability, confirmed not only by scores but by teachers, plus mixed performance." He said that when Hargadon reads comments like those, "his experience gives him a sense of what parts of the folder he should read very carefully and perhaps reread before deciding on this one. On a kid like this, Hargadon's likely to go back to his memory of other kids he had and how they did and what was the difference and where he might find the reassuring angle."

A third example illustrated how even after reading everything in a candidate's folder, the reader can be at a loss as to what to say, much less what to recommend. The example Noya gave was of a candidate who had written an essay that sounded "bleak." "There also was a teacher," he recalled, "who sort of made a reference that might also have meant that."

Sort of? Might have?

"Yeah," said Noya. "That's what you usually get. Who the hell knows?"

In a difficult case like this, what does the reader say?

"In the case I'm thinking of," Noya said, "this was a young woman with very strong credentials. Scores were very good. The program was at a good school which is considered demanding. There was no question that this girl could more than do the work at Princeton. On the personal side, it was almost frightening, I wrote, how sophisticated she had become and perhaps how cynical she had gotten at such a young age." The young woman was rejected.

As Noya's plaintive question—"Who the hell knows?"—suggests, trying to get a fix on a candidate from the application can be extremely difficult. Hargadon facetiously says his staff should wear T-shirts bearing the slogan, "We Do Precision Guesswork," and that at the top of his office stationery should be printed the words of Samuel Butler: "Life is the art of drawing sufficient conclusions from insufficient premises."

Facetious or not, that's hardly a ringing endorsement of the system by which America's top universities select America's top students. In an essay entitled "The Uses and Misuses of Tests," Diane Ravitch, a non-resident senior fellow at the Brookings Institution and an assistant secretary of education in the Bush administration, describes some of the present system's shortcomings. "Personal recommendations today carry far less weight than they once did, because letter writers can no longer rely on the confidentiality of their statements. . . . Personal interviews are helpful, but they are limited in value by the interviewer's prejudices and the student's ability to present himself."

Ravitch will get no disagreement from the people in the trenches. Terry Cowdrey of Vanderbilt says that in 95 out of

100 letters of recommendation that Vanderbilt receives, "what we read is what we already know from the grades and test scores." Vanderbilt has been known to get the exact same teacher's letter of recommendation for three or four different applicants.

It is because every indicator seems to have some sort of built-in flaw that the admissions departments of selective universities use so many of them. The theory runs, the more puzzle pieces there are to work with, the better the chances of piecing together an accurate, lifelike portrait of the candidate.

Nevertheless, Duke's Christoph Guttentag says it takes imagination to be a good dean of admissions, "the imagination to create an image of an individual in your mind." Hargadon says it takes instinct based on "life experience." Asked whether an admissions dean simply knows a good applicant when he sees one, Hargadon replies, "There's a lot to that."

At Pomona College, the second reader's job is to give what dean of admissions Bruce Poch calls a "gut reaction" to the applicant. Poch concedes that the process may appear "a little capricious." But while Ravitch argues that standardized tests, though flawed, are the fairest way to evaluate, Poch echoes other deans of admissions when he says, "You can't do it by the numbers alone."

To be sure, deans of admissions believe test scores should be part of the admissions process. Despite his own "modest" scores, Hargadon told his Princeton Club of Philadelphia audience, "I'm a defender of tests. There was a language teacher at Lower Merion who never gave A's. At least, I never found anybody who got one. Other departments, you found a lot of A's." Hargadon added that test scores also served as a "caution." "Test scores are like lights that go off (and say to me) 'Fred, do you know you are about to turn down a student who got five 800s?' "

Reed College's admissions head, Bob Mansueto, sees even more value in test scores. He says they help him to find the student who is "intellectually bursting at the seams. His school doesn't know what to do with him," thus his grades aren't always the best.

Duke's Christoph Guttentag added that test scores give deans significant information about a student's analytical abilities. However, "in and of themselves, they don't say anything about a student's insight, creativity, ability to lead a discussion, or thoughtful articulation of ideas."

Pomona's Poch provides the logical next step to Guttentag's position when he says the education offered by America's thirty to forty most selective universities truly is a better education precisely because of things that can't be measured in numbers, especially students' intellectual interests. "A young person's political and analytical thinking," he says, "is very much affected by the range of people he or she talks to over dinner for four years."

Poch's seemingly logical argument, however, leaves one with a truly illogical situation: the better the education offered by a university, the more flaws there are built into its process for selecting students.

☐   ☐   ☐   ❙   ☐

Getting back to the Princeton process, after an application has been read by three different members of the admissions staff, the applications of candidates still in the running are scrutinized by a final committee. Before Hargadon became dean of admissions, a Princeton applicant had a designated advocate who spoke on his behalf at the committee meeting. Hargadon eliminated the designated advocate—a move that, according to Noya, caused the readers to do a more thorough job. "People realized that they were not going to be in there discussing the case, so they had better write everything down."

Shortly before Hargadon arrived at Princeton, the university admitted an imposter. It took two years before the charade was exposed, not by the university, but by someone who knew the man's real identity. "I hate to tell you how few comments were [written] about that candidate," Hargadon says.

Hargadon believes that relying on the written cards instead of a designated advocate is better for the applicant because it gives the applicant three potential advocates in the committee meeting, each of whom may highlight different strengths. It also gives the committee a better chance to get at a candidate's subjective qualities, he believes.

Before Hargadon became dean, every candidate to Princeton had to fall into a category: leader, athlete, minority. The phrase used around the admissions office was, "What's the candidate's hook?" Doing it that way, Hargadon says, meant that "interstitial" candidates got overlooked. "The interstitial candidate is not going to stand out in any of these areas in which people think you get in by but will stand out as a human being; will probably end up being the person who keeps a college together or a dorm together; who, for reasons that have to do with what we sense about the person as a person, seems to have the sense of balance, the sense of perspective."

As at Rice, final decisions at Princeton are made by very few top people. But it's Hargadon who has the final responsibility for the class.

CHAPTER 8

Under Hargadon's grueling grading system, there appeared to be little question that Joshua Hastings was an academic "one."

Since Josh wanted to be an engineering student, his proficiency in math, I assumed, would inflate his stock. Not that Josh was one-dimensional academically. He had scored a 720 on his SAT verbal, plus a 760 on his Spanish achievement test, to go along with his perfect eight hundreds on the math SAT, math achievement, and physics achievement tests—not forgetting his perfect five on the advanced-placement calculus test, which he took when he was in tenth grade.

Still, I didn't think Josh was a sure bet, because his nonacademic rating was surely low. When Josh was in sixth grade, he wrote a computer program for a handicapped student that helped that student learn mathematics. But he never followed it up, and neither his parents nor his teachers nor his school counselors ever thought to suggest he expand upon that singular accomplishment and see where his natural ability and curiosity might take him.

As it was, Josh's only nonacademic achievement, if you

could call it that, was that he was a section leader in his high school marching band. No sports. No class office. Not even president of some school club. On paper Josh was a nerd. Edith Warnock, Josh's hired counselor, was going to have to work hard to make him appealing, and from their first meeting she wasn't sure she was up to the task. Josh had sat sullen and uncommunicative on her living-room couch, resentful that his mother had called in an outsider. At one point he put his shoe up on the coffee table, and his mother knocked it off. Oh, Lord, thought Warnock, what have I got here.

I thought Sirrka Romanski's chances also looked good even though it was still too soon to know whether her grades would hold up in her new high school. It wasn't likely that Hargadon would come across a lot of candidates who were personally familiar with the war in Bosnia and Herzegovina. If I was interested in knowing Sirrka's views on the war, I figured Hargadon might be, too, through Sirrka's essay.

Meanwhile, nothing I had learned about the Princeton admissions process gave me reason to be optimistic about Lucy Simmons's chances. Other than in math, Lucy's test scores were below 700. They weren't much below; they just were consistently below. Yes, she had taken the hard courses and gotten A's. But her high school was only average. And if being class president made a candidate only a nonacademic three, then being president of the Key Club and the Computer Club probably made Lucy a four.

Just as Josh hadn't been encouraged to develop his special interest in computers, Lucy hadn't been encouraged to develop her fascination with psychology, which she was exposed to as a freshman when she took a psych course on her own.

Ironically, Josh's high school offered psychology courses. But when Lucy tried to get her high school to offer a psychology course, she was rebuffed. Nowhere did I see where Lucy had done something trailblazing, like start a chamber orchestra or increase the circulation of her school newspaper eightfold. Neither did Lucy have a savvy guidance counselor to fall back on. All told, it seemed to me that Lucy's best chance of getting in was to come across as a likable, interactive candidate, which I genuinely felt she was. And since by coincidence I had been randomly selected by the alumni committee to be her interviewer, maybe I was in a position to make a difference.

How important is it for an applicant to hook up with a good alumni interviewer? Once in a great while, it can make all the difference in the world. As reported in the alumni magazine, several years ago a young woman applied to Princeton who had great grades her freshman and senior year of high school. But for some reason that wasn't explained on her application, she had done lousy in both her sophomore and junior years. On the face of it, the girl stood very little chance of being admitted. But when she started talking to her alumni interviewer, the story emerged of a young woman whose mother had been dying of cancer, who had had to clean the house and cook the meals and keep herself from going to pieces while trying to keep up with her schoolwork. So moved was the alumna that she urged the admissions department to take a second look at this candidate, which it did, and the girl was admitted.

The alumni interviewer's report is almost never the determining factor, Hargadon stresses, but if it's informative, it becomes another piece of the puzzle. In some cases the report becomes what Hargadon calls the "exclamation point," the confirmation of the admissions department's assessment of the applicant. In a cover letter to the handbook for alumni interviewers, Princeton's Schools Committee chairperson wrote: "Informative and timely interview reports provide an additional dimension, sometimes a critical one, to an applicant's file."

"*Sometimes critical.*" If I were to help Lucy in my interviewer's report, I would have to convey the nuances that made her stand out.

▢ ▢ ▢ ▮ ▢

Since Lucy was an early action candidate, we met one fall night at her suburban home, about a two-hour drive from the Princeton campus. She greeted me at the front door wearing a very proper dark dress, then shook my hand and rather stiffly asked me to come in. She escorted me downstairs to the shag-carpeted family room. A pot of hot coffee was waiting on the table in front of the sofa. As I poured, her two small dogs came bounding down the stairs, raced across the room, and jumped up in her lap. Lucy and I laughed. The ice was broken.

After she finally got the dogs under control, Lucy said she hadn't laughed so hard since she went bowling the other night. When I said that bowling isn't something that makes most people laugh, she said what else could she do after bowling an eight.

"You mean in one frame?" I asked.

"No!" she said with mock horror. "That was my score for the entire game!"

"Oooh," I said. "That really is pathetic."

"The sad part is, I was really trying."

Then, perhaps fearing that she was sounding silly—which she wasn't—Lucy turned serious and said, "I can explain the physics of baseball to you. I can explain the physics of pool."

"Okay," I said, and for a while we talked about why curve balls curve and why eight balls spin. I didn't understand a word she was saying, but I didn't want to stop her because she was really into it. I tried to imagine how I would react to Lucy if I were her classmate at Princeton. It struck me that she was friendly and outgoing, just the sort who would fit into the Princeton community.

After she finished telling me why she would make a great baseball pitching coach, I asked her about extracurricular activities. She thought for a while, then said, "I guess what I'm most proud of is my tutoring." Her comment impressed me since I hadn't asked what activity gave her the most personal satisfaction. When I asked why she was so proud, she described a boy she had tutored in math when he was a senior and she was just a sophomore. The boy had been failing trigonometry when a teacher asked Lucy to help out. Lucy worked with him after school, and slowly he started getting the hang of it. "You should have seen his face light up when he started understanding what it was all about," Lucy said, teary-eyed. "I still can't get over how good that made me feel."

It made me feel good just listening to her, a feeling I continued to have when I asked her what she had put down on her Princeton application under "favorite quotation." Lucy said she had used some lines from a sonnet by Shakespeare:

Love is not
Which alters when it alteration finds,
Or tends with the remover to remove.

When I asked, a bit indelicately, what that meant, she did not get defensive or indignant. Instead, she opened up to me about how those lines of poetry captured her own feelings about love, which she then did her best to explain. That Lucy would let down her guard like that with a total stranger said to me that she had poise and maturity and wasn't afraid to be herself.

The next night, while everything was still fresh in my mind, I sat down in front of a typewriter and filled out my report. I immediately made a mistake that, in retrospect, might have caused Hargadon to write off my report as worthless.

Thinking that I needed to stand up for Lucy, I discussed her grades and test scores—something that, had I first read my copy of the interviewer's handbook that had recently arrived in the mail, I would have known not to do, because all that information is already clear from the transcript. I wrote, "Lucy's high school is no academic hotbed. Her math board scores are indicative of extraordinary natural talent."

I made matters worse by failing to simply describe how the conversation went, so that Hargadon could feel as if he were sharing the front porch with me. Instead, I used formal, lifeless language to describe how I felt: "Lucy will be the one who organizes academic bull sessions in her dorm. She will invigorate everyone around her."

I still wasn't finished mucking things up. In answering the

question about what a Princeton professor might expect of this applicant, I made Lucy sound like someone who doesn't ever fall or stumble, and hence she didn't seem real. I wrote, "Expect a tough, inquisitive student who'll jumpstart every precept she's in and continue the discussion well into the night over a pot of coffee in her dorm room."

What a yawn.

At the end of my report, in the space provided for my overall assessment of the applicant, I kept Lucy a marble statue on a wooden pedestal. Lucy, I wrote, has "an inner confidence that fosters an intense curiosity about everything about her, plus a wonderful, self-deprecating sense of humor."

My report on Lucy was the sort of report any parent would love to have someone write about his or her child. That was the problem: I had written my report like a parent, not like the journalist the handbook says I'm supposed to be—and which, ironically, by profession, I am.

When I finally got around to reading the five reports included in the handbook under "Examples of Useful Interview Reports," I discovered that what makes a report really good is simply one of the fundamentals of good writing—using material that brings the subject to life. Each of these five actual reports was essentially a cinematic treatment of the applicant that put the reader in the middle of the picture. Each told an interesting story—a good yarn, as Huckleberry Finn might have said—that got below the surface to the "real" candidate, exposing his warts as well as his warmth.

To be sure, it helps when the interviewer has an exceptional candidate to write about. One interviewer commented after being dazzled by a candidate named Paul, "A saber-fencing potter who summers in Spain? This is why I do interviews! What a delight to meet and talk with someone with this unusual mix of talents, interests, and experiences."

Paul, the interviewer informed Hargadon, reads a lot outside of his school assignments, including, most recently, *The Periodic Table,* a novel recommended to him by his father, who is a doctor. Paul also is into Japanese pottery; he doesn't just read about it, he makes it on his own potter's wheel. The interviewer also had found what former Princeton admissions staffer Roberto Noya called the "reassuring angle"—a reason for Hargadon not to worry about something which, if it popped up elsewhere in Paul's folder, might cause him to worry. In Paul's case, the problem was that he was introverted. Paul was not "a particularly game conversationalist," the interviewer wrote, but added that when their conversation reached a deeper, more philosophical level, Paul opened up. When the interviewer asked Paul to describe one of the pots he had made, he said: "A respect for tradition. Not trying to be extreme or eccentric." In describing himself, Paul was equally insightful: "It's not meaningful if you have to fit into other situations instead of being yourself."

It also helps the interviewer when a candidate has a great project. "When I asked her about her proudest achievements, the answer impressed me," one interviewer wrote about a girl named Janice. "Remembering that this girl is valedictorian, state writing champion, etc., she said that the thing that she took most pride in was making the literary magazine something that 'wasn't just for nerds anymore,' but was appealing to all classes of students, including athletes. This showed me a talent for leadership in an academic pursuit, and the ability to be an appealing example to others. But it also demonstrated her gift for verbal communication. She explained this source of pride in a way that made it come alive to me."

This interviewer continued that "during sophomore and especially junior year, [Janice] worked hard on increasing the magazine's attraction. She spoke to classes, designed posters, and sought out and encouraged potential contributors. Outside of school she went to banks, businesses, and the school board, in order to raise more money to improve the magazine. Not only was the magazine able to overcome its 'chronic lack of money,' it raised enough to go to a better quality paper, plus acquired the ability to shrink and expand illustrations and photos. 'This year we hope to go to color,' she said. The staff of the magazine was about eight to nine students her freshman year. By the end of last year, her first as editor, the staff had increased to about twenty. In addition, she takes special pride in the fact that the work is no longer exclusively contributed by staff members. She said, 'We've gotten some great poetry from a guy who up to then was known only for math,' and another submission from an athlete. You could see on her face and in the tone of her voice how pleased she was to have played a large role in taking the literary magazine from its former narrow base to a broader popularity."

In summarizing Janice, the interviewer wrote, "a perfect person."

Perfect definitely was not the word that another interviewer used to describe a candidate named Nat. But the interviewer described the young man's faults in such a way as to make Nat seem like a real and likable person, for whom Princeton would be a good match.

Asked for his first impression of Nat, the interviewer wrote, "When I arrived at his house, Nat, attired in sweats, apparently had forgotten what time we were supposed to meet and was surprised to see me so early! However, he agreed to the interview then and did not become flustered."

Later in his report, the interviewer wrote: "I also asked Nat to discuss his strengths and weaknesses with me. He prides himself on his 'adaptability' and his 'ability to pick things up quickly.' However, he also admits to being somewhat lazy and disorganized."

In summarizing his impressions of Nat, the interviewer gave Hargadon a reassuring angle. "I am confident," the interviewer concluded, "that Nat has the intelligence to effectively handle the coursework at Princeton, particularly based upon his past academic performance. On the other hand, Nat himself recognizes his capacity to be lazy and disorganized. Based upon my short meeting with Nat, I can see how these tendencies might cause difficulties later on in college. However, given that these tendencies have apparently not hindered his past academic performance, I don't expect that they would significantly affect future performance, especially given his eagerness to embrace greater academic challenges."

The report on Nat effectively highlighted his strengths. Commenting on Nat's extracurricular activities, the interviewer wrote that in addition to several after-school activities, "Nat also works one day a week at J.C. Penney. He enjoys his part-time job because he is a 'floater,' meaning that he is randomly assigned to a department each night. Nat finds this more challenging because he's never sure exactly where he'll be and he's forced to learn very quickly about a department when he is assigned there."

Nat's whimsicality also came through in the report. Asked to name one of the most difficult challenges he has faced, Nat told the interviewer that "he was finally successful in solving a video computer game called Zork II after about two years."

▯ ▯ ▯ ▮ ▯

Reading these reports made me realize that my effort on behalf of Lucy had missed the mark, but I could take comfort that Lucy at least had an alumni report. When Hargadon got around to reading Josh Hastings's folder, he wasn't going to find an alumni report at all.

It wasn't as if Josh lived far away from the nearest interviewer. On the contrary, there had to be a dozen interviewers within a stone's throw of Josh's suburban Connecticut home. Nor was it that Josh didn't want an interview, which some candidates don't. On the contrary, when Josh's interviewer unexpectedly canceled at the last minute, his mother worked hard to arrange another. Alice called a friend who did interviews, but the friend thought it would be better if Josh talked to someone he didn't know. So the friend gave Alice another alumnus to call, and she got on the phone and all but pleaded with this gentleman to interview her son. The alum, however, didn't want to be bothered, so he talked her out of it by telling her that the alumni interviewer's report doesn't count for anything—after all, he said, none of his own interviewees had ever been admitted.

In Josh's case, the absence of an alumni interviewer's report was potentially significant since his great academic record, but almost nonexistent extracurricular record, left him looking one-dimensional.

He wasn't the only one in this predicament. Typically, for one reason or another, roughly forty percent of Princeton candidates do not get interviewed by an alumnus or alumna. "A significant fraction of our applications," Hargadon later wrote, "make an additional round of reviews precisely because, in the absence of an ASC [alumni interviewer's] report, I am likely to write on the folder, 'Would like to see what ASC's impressions of this candidate are.'"

Josh had three other reports in his folder—two teachers' and a guidance counselor's—plus his own essay. He could only hope that it would be enough.

CHAPTER ▯ 9

As he was riding in a car on a California freeway, the cool winter air was blowing in Mark Ghani's face. At the wheel was the middle-aged Princeton alumnus who had been assigned to interview him. As they zipped along, the alum told Mark to look at the back seat. He turned and did a double-take. A stun gun, the alum casually remarked, comes in handy these days on California freeways. Mark started to wonder what he had gotten himself into.

When they reached the alum's office, he showed Mark a jar filled with fluid and something murkily solid. The jar contained a two-headed animal fetus that he had come across during his work, he told his young guest. At this point Mark was ready to head for the exit. But not wanting to do anything that might screw up his chances for admission, he reluctantly stayed, and for the next several minutes he listened to the alum talk—mostly just about himself. Mark had a clear view of the jar over the alum's shoulder during this monologue. When the session was finally over, the alum, who still knew almost nothing about Mark, told him he would think of something positive to write about him.

Unfortunately for Mark, this was not the first time life had been a puzzle.

☐ ☐ ☐ **▌** ☐

Mark Ghani is a tall thin boy, with high protruding cheek-bones, a very long narrow nose, and brown eyes set close together under thin straight brows. His short brown hair is always neatly combed, and he dresses more formally than most of his southern California classmates, preferring pants in keeping with an English boarding school to the bright patterned shorts that are more the norm among his peers.

Mark lives in a neighborhood of one hundred or so houses on the side of a hill in an upper-middle-class suburb several miles outside Los Angeles. All the homes, including Mark's, have small sloping front yards, white stucco sides, and red Spanish tile roofs. Several doctors, including Mark's father, live in the neighborhood, whose streets bear "Residents Only" signs. Private security guards patrol after dark. Although the area is mostly white, his neighbors include prosperous Asian, Indian, and Pakistani families like his own. The loudest neighborhood noises are the false alarms of home security systems. The neighbors wave to each other, but there are never any block parties.

Mark's house has a big entry area that opens directly onto a living room with a cathedral ceiling. The room is dominated by a large abstract portrait, the dominant color of which is bright blue. A baby grand piano takes up a lot of the floor space. The brass lamps are antiques, as are the picture frames, which contain family photos. The upstairs study holds the family computer.

One summer when Mark was still small, his father bought flash cards and told him to go to his room and learn the multiplication tables. Mark dutifully obeyed, but try as he might, he couldn't get the hang of it, much to his father's frustration.

Just as football coach Vince Lombardi preached that "winning isn't everything, it's the *only* thing," Mark's father drummed into him that education is "number one" at all times. When Mark was only five, his father regularly sat him on his knee and read him the news briefs from the front page of *The Wall Street Journal.* When young Mark would watch a documentary on public television, his father would say, "Watch very carefully. I'm going to ask you questions." In elementary school, when Mark brought home his report card, his father would highlight all his areas of supposed deficiency—supposed because, except for math, Mark always did extremely well in school. He was also pursuing music, dutifully practicing his violin.

A couple of summers after the incident with the multiplication tables, Mark's father brought home a math workbook and told him, "You owe me four lessons a day by the time I get home." A summer or two after that, Mark's father, for reasons of his own, decided that his son should learn how to type.

Midway through Mark's ninth-grade year, his older brother was accepted by Harvard. Suddenly Mark's father imposed a new goal: He must do as well as his older brother. He, too, must go to Harvard. Nothing less would do.

As a sophomore, Mark started attending a "magnet" high school—actually a school within a school—for gifted students, housed in a building that also housed an inner-city high school. Coming from his suburb, Mark found his new surroundings physically intimidating; but that fear was nothing compared with the intimidation he felt in his tenth-grade classroom. After years of being an academic ace in everyone's eyes but his parents', he was "slaughtered," he says. "Slaughtered" means that he got a couple of A's, a couple of B's, and a C or two—not bad for most kids, but not nearly good enough for someone who absolutely had to get into Harvard.

Mark and his parents alike went off the deep end. One time when he had a big biology project due, Mark went up to his room and, rather than get down to work, drew pictures, then simply went to sleep. "I was really depressed," he said. His mother sent him to a psychologist, who gave him a series of tests and told him that his problem was lack of self-esteem. It was time for him to stop comparing himself with his older brother, she said. It was time for him to ease up on the pressure. She urged him to set his sights on an easier college.

Mark didn't take kindly to her advice. "I was mad at her. Incensed, really," he says, especially at the part about lowering his sights. Yet for reasons Mark never understood, his father began to treat him differently, substituting support for discipline. One night at the dinner table, he told his son that it was more important for him to be himself than to be number one. By now, however, Mark had but one thing on his mind: "I wanted to just run away." And so Mark took off for four months to a place as far away as he could get—Singapore—as part of a student-exchange program. He left before the end of his sophomore year, and he didn't come back until after his junior year had started.

Being a sixteen-year-old on his own in a foreign country, Mark says, "was really scary and loads of fun." Most of all, however, it was a learning experience. As a student in a Singaporean school, Mark observed a much more demanding system, in which certain standardized tests were given every couple of years. Do badly on "one test, and you can be gone" from school, Mark notes, your plans for the future crushed. As he watched his schoolmates frantically prepare for their make-or-break tests, he thought: "Here, people's whole lives depend on how hard they work. To know that I'm capable of it and not do it is ridiculous."

Mark returned home "completely changed" by his experience, he says. He was going to work hard in school—not because his father wanted him to but because he wanted to. Even as he returned for his junior year in high school, however, he already felt defeated by the specter of Harvard. "I didn't want to think if I tried my hardest I still wouldn't be able to do it."

What else had not changed was Mark's lack of self-confidence in math. Even though he knew it would look bad on a college application, he couldn't bring himself to take another math course.

Otherwise, Mark had a great junior year academically. He took the hardest subjects, got straight A's, and even scored a perfect five on the AP test in European history. He decided to hold off on taking the SATs until the fall of his senior year, so that in the interim he could somehow make up his deficiency in math. He became head of his school's student-exchange program chapter, worked as a laboratory assistant at a hospital, and tutored other students in English.

Then there occurred what can only be described as a "serendipitous" chain of events.

During the entire span of his very stressful childhood, no matter how depressed he got, Mark had never stopped playing the violin. He had taken refuge in music. "It was the one thing that made me feel worthwhile." Not that he worked at it—playing the violin just came naturally. After he returned from Singapore, however, Mark wanted to take it more seriously. So after ten years with the same violin teacher, Mark sought out another, tougher teacher. The one he decided on usually didn't take on high school students, but after a lot of nagging, she agreed to teach him. Then she proceeded to tell him that he played as if he had been taking lessons for only five years. If you really want to get better, she told him, go to a certain summer music camp in Michigan.

After junior year Mark accepted the challenge, only to find himself surrounded by extraordinarily gifted violinists. All were locked in competition over who would be in the camp's top orchestra. Mark found himself on the spot: Like all the others, he had to perform in front of his peers, who would then vote in a secret ballot to rank the players. This ranking process went on day after day. For Mark it was excruciatingly painful—but it was also intoxicating. He practiced eight hours a day, seven days a week. He made it into the second violin section of the top orchestra, but even after he was comfortably ensconced there, he kept up his grueling practice schedule. He actually came to love the intense effort. "If you really work at something," he discovered, "eventually you'll be able to do it."

When Mark started his senior year, he competed as he always had for the first chair in his high school orchestra. For the first time ever, Mark won.

That same September, Mark had to make some serious choices about college. One night he and his parents sat around the kitchen table, Mom with pen and paper, weighing which colleges Mark should apply to. One thing was certain: Harvard was everybody's first choice. It had always been his parents' favorite. Mark had made Harvard his number-one choice based on his successful junior year and because, when he visited his brother there, he had had a great time in the dorm and had participated in class discussions.

As a West Coast kid, Mark knew about few colleges other than Harvard and the various branches of the University of California. His mother, who had grown up back east, suggested that he apply to the other top Ivies, too, which in her opinion were Yale, Princeton, Dartmouth, and Brown. Mom and Dad suggested he apply to Stanford, as well as the University of California at Berkeley, UCLA, and, as a backup, UC Irvine.

Mark had a problem with the inclusion of Princeton on this list. "New Jersey's ugly," he told his parents. When Mom said the Princeton area of New Jersey was really quite pretty, Mark shrugged. "Okay. What the hell," he said.

Mark decided to take an extra heavy courseload in the fall of his senior year. Again there was no math, but he took advanced-placement English, psychology, economics, government, and history. Mark's folks were surprised—they had thought he might lighten up a bit because, after all, senior year was supposed to be a time to have fun. Indeed, a number of Mark's classmates in the gifted program decided not to take

AP courses, even though they had heard via the grapevine that that would hurt their chances at the most selective schools. They had decided not even to try to get into those universities and instead set their sights on UCLA and Berkeley, fine colleges that, according to high school lore, accepted in-state students as long as they pulled A's in non-AP courses.

The critical academic moment of Mark's fall came in October, when he took the SATs. By normal standards, Mark's 610 in math was very good. Considering his background, it was fantastic. Still, for a candidate to an elite Ivy school like Harvard, 610 was hardly impressive. His 750 on the verbal test was an obvious plus, but still, there would be candidates with higher verbal scores than that.

Mark crossed his fingers and sent in his Harvard application as part of the early action program. Princeton would have to wait.

CHAPTER □ **10**

Thanksgiving was just another workday for Princeton's dean of admissions. Before leaving his house, Hargadon set his VCR to record the Stanford football game, to be televised later that day. Around midday, he took a couple of hours off to have dinner with his elderly mother, who lived not far away, but after dinner and a quick look-see at the pro game on TV, he headed back to the office, back to reading the 2,000 early action applications.

Though Hargadon and his staff had started reading the early action folders only about three weeks ago, in just another week or two the letters would have to be posted informing each candidate whether he or she had been accepted, rejected, or "deferred" until the regular action period in the spring. Adding to the pressure, the staff wasn't yet at full strength. The new staffers weren't yet completely trained, and some were still on the road.

This year, about 600 of Princeton's early action candidates were going to be admitted. That would leave just 1,400 letters of acceptance for the more than 12,000 applicants in the spring pool, which would include those deferred from the fall.

Clearly, a greater percentage of early action than regular applicants are accepted. Such statistics are familiar to many high school juniors and seniors and their supporters, some of whom interpret them to mean that applying early will improve their chances of getting in. This is another myth, however, just like the myth that admissions departments take only a few minutes to make up their minds about an applicant.

The higher percentage of fall acceptances reflects not better odds but the advantages that money can buy. Early action candidates tend to be students at the best public and independent high schools and have guidance counselors who give them lots of assistance. "For candidates to have taken all their tests, be organized, get it all in—a disproportionate number of them are really top candidates," according to Hargadon.

Still, how can the dean be sure he won't see a lot of even stronger candidates in the spring? Experience, Hargadon says—some three decades' worth—tells him that the candidates he admits in the fall are unlikely to be surpassed by those he will see in the spring. To be sure, Hargadon and his lieutenants will defer a number of great-looking fall candidates precisely because they can't be sure a spring candidate won't be even a little better. But sometimes that even-better candidate doesn't come along, which is why one hundred or more deferred applicants may be admitted on the second go-round.

Like everything else in the admissions process, early action is a balancing act: an elite university wants to offer early admission to as many as possible because they may—or have to, in the case of early decision—commit to enrolling before they've heard from the other schools. At the same time, an elite university wants as strong a class as possible, and experience says that the applications of many fantastic applicants won't arrive until just after January 1. Indeed, some great applicants will be applying early elsewhere and won't get in, turning them off that other institution and on to Princeton.

A myth has grown up that *every* candidate has a one-in-six or one-in-seven chance of being offered admission, as calculated by taking (as *U.S. News & World Report* does) the total number of acceptances offered and dividing that number by the total number of students who apply. "There's no candidate I meet that I can tell them the odds are one out of six, because the odds aren't one out of six for everybody. Some candidates have a one-out-of-two chance, some a one out of forty," Hargadon says, adding that the last student admitted in the spring had just as much chance of being the strongest candidate in the entire applicant pool as the first kid admitted in the fall.

Three of my five student subjects applied early to Princeton: Josh, Sirrka, and Lucy. Mark applied early to Harvard. Would all of them make it? Would any of them? Were any of them destined to join a select group that included the young woman who had been president of her class for two consecutive years and captain of the cheerleading squad, had scored a 730 on the SAT verbal and a 760 on the SAT math, a 740 on the English achievement test, and a 700 on the math achievement test? One of the school reports on her noted that she was the "most outstanding student" in twenty-two years. Another said, "The best we've ever graduated."

To be sure, not even such laudatory comments are a guarantee of admission. "Do you know how many times I read,

'Best student I've had in ten years,' 'Best math student in twenty years'? How many times?!" Hargadon asks plaintively. "I'd be shocked if I was some of the kids that I turn down."

▯ ▯ ▯ ▮ ▯

With Josh, Sirrka, and Lucy, I couldn't help but think that success or failure might all come down to the essays they had written.

"In the space below," the Princeton directions read, "tell one story about yourself that would best provide us, either directly or indirectly, with an insight into the kind of person you are. For example, the story can simply relate a personal experience, or a humorous anecdote; it can tell about an especially significant academic encounter or about an unusual test of character. The possibilities are unlimited (well, almost so). You choose. Just relax and write it."

While some prestigious institutions use the essay primarily as an indicator of the applicant's quality of thinking, Hargadon, to borrow a phrase from Toni Morrison, the Nobel Prize–winning author who teaches creative writing at Princeton, also uses it as a "rip in the tent," through which he squeezes to get to that "real" person lying beneath the idealized surface created by grades and test scores.

"What interests me the most in the work I do here," Morrison once told a group of fellow African-American educators at Princeton, "is the thirst among students and faculty, but especially among students—black students, white students—for . . . a vocabulary that allows them to talk about race in a manner that is not diminishing, demeaning, reductive or *ad hominem*. Race is a very difficult thing to talk about, because the conversation frequently ends up being patronizing, guilt ridden, hostile, or resentful. But for those of us interested in the study of literature and the writing of literature, it is something they have to confront and think about. Without this language, you can't produce new knowledge, you can only refigure what you already know."

Hargadon, too, is very concerned about the artful use of language. Shortly after he arrived at Princeton, he summarized his thoughts in a letter to guidance counselors remarking on "just how tricky is this business of language we use to communicate with each other, just how variable can be the meanings of the same word, and how differently intentioned can be the use of words even when there is no disagreement over their precise meaning."

Hargadon had sent a memo to his staff, he told the counselors, in which he quoted from Flaubert: "Whatever the thing you wish to say, there is but one word to express it, but one verb to give it movement, but one adjective to qualify it; you must seek until you find this noun, this verb, this adjective. When you pass a grocer sitting in his doorway, a porter smoking a pipe, or a cab stand, show me that grocer and that porter . . . in such a way that I could not mistake them for any other grocer or porter, and by a single word give me to understand wherein the cab horse differs from fifty others before it or behind it."

And so understandably, at Princeton as at other elite universities, an applicant's essay often winds up being the focal point of his folder because it demonstrates several important things at once: the quality of the student's thinking, the skill with which he communicates, and the person behind the grades and test scores.

Josh wrote an essay that nobody could have told him to write—a story that came from both his heart and his head. To be sure, Josh probably wouldn't have been so creative if Edith Warnock, his hired counselor, hadn't encouraged him. Though Warnock originally thought Josh was a pain in the rear, after a couple of sessions she started seeing him as a warm and funny, if slightly arrogant, young man. Her strategy was to take advantage of Josh's streak of arrogance by encouraging him to write about absolutely anything he wanted to, knowing that he would be secure enough to do just that.

Josh wrote a story about an incident in his life that I subsequently titled "The Jiffy Pop Ritual."

The only reason that my friends and I were not pronounced clinically insane long ago is that the clinic doesn't want to admit that there are cases as bad as us floating around. We enjoy doing things just because they are so completely unexpected. Take the Jiffy Pop ritual, for example.

Jiffy Pop popcorn comes in a disc-shaped aluminum container and is intended to be placed on top of a stove to pop. But that's too easy! Where's the challenge? Real men would never make popcorn like that! Real men would take this Jiffy Pop into a park in the dead of night, find a grill, light a fire, burn old coloring books for fuel, and cook their Jiffy Pop there! Needless to say, my friends and I are real men. (That's one of the nicer things we've been called. "Beyond help" is much more common.) We cook our Jiffy Pop the way it was intended to be cooked. Once, however, the insanity of this ritual led us to another kind of insanity, slightly more hazardous to our health. One site of the ritual could only be accessed by driving along the 0.8 mile track that looped around the park. Normally, this is no problem, although the track is only wide enough for cars to drive in one direction. However, night makes it difficult, and rain makes it even more so.

For exactly this reason, my friend Wilhelm (the names have been changed to protect the innocent . . . and the guilty, whose parents still don't know this happened) was wondering just how fast he could take the loop. Of course, we were not so stupid as to floor it and find out. I had studied Physics, so I was able to inform the inquisitive Wilhelm. I knew that turning a car was a function of friction, and friction was given by the formula $F = \mu_k N$. The fact that $N = F_{grav} = mg$ and m_{car} was about 1500 kg helped increase the maximum velocity greatly, but the fact that the μ_k for wet pavement is equal to about 0.10 forces the car to move more slowly. $\mu_k m_{car} g = (0.10)(1500 \text{ kg})(9.8 \text{ m/sec}^2) = 1470 \text{ N}$, not much in terms of a 1983 Chevy Citation. This has to be equal to the centripetal force, $m_{car} V^2 / R_{track}$. The radius of the track was about 100 meters. $1470 \text{ N} = (1500) V^2 / (100)$ reduces to $V \approx 9.9 \text{ m/s}$, about 22 mph. Wilhelm had pulled over so I could make my calculations, and I was quite satisfied with my results when I told him the answer. Wilhelm, however, was worried that I had made a mistake somewhere, and insisted on checking the calculations by experiment. I agreed that it was possible that I had made a mistake somewhere, so I was forced to concede that a verifying experiment would be worthwhile. This was performed by Wilhelm, with me riding shotgun. As the car was rounding the curve at 40, I began to doubt my calculations. However, I was vindicated when at the last moment, the car skidded off the track and was stopped by a force of 3.8×10^4 N exerted over 0.7 seconds by a large tree. Fortunately, no one was hurt, but the car was totaled as the kinetic energy of the car ($\frac{1}{2}mv^2 = 2.4 \times 10^5$ Joules) was converted into car-wrecking energy.

This sad incident taught me to trust my own calculations only when I understand what I am doing. It also taught me to double-check my work, because after a little thought I realized that with one slip of an exponent, I could have easily told Wilhelm that doing 70 would be fine, in which case we would have had to hit 90 to test the theoretical answer. It was also demonstrated that Jiffy Popping and driving greatly increases one's chances of having an accident. (Although I admit that only having one instance is minimal data, the hypothesis is consistent with known facts.) Most importantly, however, Wilhelm and I confirmed a number of key formulas of classical mechanics.

I had the distinct feeling that Josh's essay was going to stand him in good stead with Hargadon. I had the same feeling when I started reading Sirrka's essay, the first paragraph of which made me think that I was about to share something very personal, very intimate—almost a religious experience.

"Every summer I return. I go back to that familiar place where I am so warmly welcomed, where I can always find a separate peace that no other home could ever fulfill. It is my refuge, my place of rejuvenation for my body, mind, and spirit. They always wait for me, and the moment I arrive it is almost as though I had never left."

The promise of intimate, personal expression got even stronger in the second paragraph.

"I am half a Yugoslavian, half an American, growing up in the United States, yet raised with very different customs and living with two different cultures. Very often I don't feel like a whole, while juggling youth and adulthood in the midst of two languages and two traditions, not as a true American nor completely Yugoslavian. Yet, always I am brought back to my special place, not by necessity or coaxing, but by a stronger, inner force that compels me to return to the ones I miss, to the place I yearn for, to the people who are my flesh and blood. With them I always feel a sense of belonging, of being with people who uphold the same values, dreams as I do. There, I understand and am understood."

By now I was dying to know: Understand what? Understood by whom? What are you like, Sirrka? Go on, tell us your story!

Instead, Sirrka began to describe the civil war in her native country. "My haven is now a battleground where a horrifying civil war has been raging for almost a year," she wrote. But instead of describing how the loss of her haven (which seemed as much a mental as a physical refuge) had personally affected her, Sirrka complained about the treatment her people were getting in the U.S. media. "Could it be," she wrote, "that the whole truth is too complex for the U.S. media? Could it be that 300 years of incessant conflicts among the Balkan rivals cannot be summarized in convenient sound bites? Could it be that American reporters receive and publicize only one side of the story, on which the public (supported by the President) then forms an opinion?"

By now, Sirrka's essay had a tinny ring to it, tinny because it had become impersonal and abstract. "This war has provided me an opportunity to evaluate what is happening in Yugoslavia from a very unique perspective—one that is both painful and rewarding." Perhaps. But what has happened to the young girl who felt caught between two continents, two cultures? Where has this essay's *feeling* gone?

I was further disappointed because I know that Sirrka had already written a wonderful essay. She volunteered at a local hospital, in part because she hoped to be a doctor someday. One day she had an experience that strengthened her resolve to one day go to medical school, and she had captured the incident in the pages of her diary the very night it happened:

> It had been just like any other Wednesday that day volunteering at the hospital . . . until one of the nurses came up to me and said, "Please tell me if you feel uncomfortable doing this, but the woman in Cubicle 2 is dying and none of her relatives or friends have come to see her. Would you mind just holding her hand and sitting with her?" . . . Lying there in front of me, curled up on a stretcher in a flimsy nightgown that exposed her frail, debilitated body, was an elderly, lonely woman gasping her last breaths of life. . . . At any second I just expected the beeping to stop and turn into that monotone lull—that beeeeeeeeeeeeep that means the heart has stopped. I didn't notice when the nurse left the room, but I remember that I just started to cry. I held her hand but I really didn't know what to say or do. . . . Somehow I just started telling her that she would soon be in a better place where she didn't have to suffer or be alone. . . . Did she hear me? I don't know. Probably not. . . . Her eyes were open but she had this far-away, sort of glazed look. . . . Her hand was withered, wrinkled, exposing each blue vein, weak, yellowed,

and limp, next to mine—young, smooth, white, and soft. This was the meaning of a lifetime—of being born and growing strong and withering away and dying. . . . I gently stroked her hand for the last time, pulled back the curtain, and said good-bye. . . . In seeing this woman's frailty, deterioration, and powerlessness, I realized my own possibilities and hopes in becoming someone who has the power to fix something that is broken, to cure something sick—to save a human life.

Lucy's essay was even more problematic. Indeed, in the first two paragraphs, she seemed itching for a fight with Hargadon for demanding that she write anything at all. This is how she began:

> When confronted with the seemingly insurmountable task of writing my essay in my application to Princeton University, I immediately panicked. After all, I supposed, Princeton would probably want some irresistible story comprised of sharp witticisms and heroic true-life tales which could only make the question of my acceptance a moot one—my application would scream out, "I am Princeton material. Take me now."
>
> Well, so sorry to disappoint, but I am not the author of any anthropological studies, I am not a prima ballerina, I have not formed my own political party and I have not volunteered at a Lepers' Colony.

Why had she started out so defensively, describing everything she was not? And how was she going to rise to the bait? What "personal experience . . . humorous anecdote . . . especially significant academic encounter . . . or unusual test of character" would she use to fulfill Princeton's request to "provide us . . . with an insight into the kind of person you are"?

Remembering that her brother had gotten into a good school after writing an essay about an animal, Lucy decided to do the same. She wrote about how she had picked out her dog at a local kennel.

> Suddenly out stumbled the most perfect vision of a puppy that I had ever dreamed of. All fur and pads flying, pencil eraser-sized nose glistening, and slightly overweight belly and backside wobbling, she was beautiful! But how could I be sure she was the one? After tripping over her oversized, over-hairy feet, she finally approached me and stopped. Without any hesitation at all, she plopped down on her back with her smooth stomach exposed and tail wagging; she was waiting for a belly rub! I pulled her onto my lap and indulged her. We became fast friends. As I lifted her up to carry her away from the kennel, I looked down and noticed that one of us had wet ourselves; knowing that I am already toilet-trained, I assumed that it was (her). We are partners for life.

> So, I apologize if I shed no light on my academic and scholastic background and achievements; I just figured that most of that was covered in the rest of my application. I just wanted to write about my dog. . . .

After reading this essay, about the only thing Hargadon was going to know about Lucy was that she was potty-trained. That, and the fact that she seemed to have a chip on her shoulder that caused her to resist following directions.

▯ ▯ ▯ ▮ ▯

Mark Ghani's essay for Harvard wasn't as sarcastic-sounding as Lucy's, but it was equally bland and stilted. Mark wrote about the first time he was sure he wanted to go to Harvard. It sounded as if it had been copied out of the university's admissions brochure. It began:

> Sitting over a plate of eggplant in a Chinese restaurant in Boston, my older brother said, "Mark, you can do this too!"
>
> It has been my dream since that week in Cambridge my sophomore year in high school to come to Harvard. It's because of Harvard's buildings, its liberal arts courses, being involved in a center of learning.

This rather pompous writing revealed almost nothing about who Mark was, what he believed in or felt. It did nothing to separate Mark from the thousands of other "qualified" applicants who could voice the same sentiments about Harvard. It was, in short, a dud. Not that Mark hadn't spent a lot of time on it. On the contrary, like Lucy, Mark had sweated over his essay, crafting half a dozen different versions. It appeared that he had worked too hard to create the "perfect" piece, meaning the one he thought Harvard would most want to read. By so doing, Mark and Lucy had violated the first commandment of essay writing: Just be yourself. They had created something generic and misplayed what could have been one of their strongest cards.

CHAPTER 11

Hargadon reaches for the letter on top of the stack that occupies the center of his desk. He scans it, chuckles, and says, "This guy deserves a personal reply." It is a letter of recommendation written by a father on behalf of his daughter. "He's a Harvard guy," Hargadon says. "Listen to how he starts off: 'I find myself in the unusual position of writing in support . . .' " Hargadon's voice trails off. He looks out the window for a moment, an idea forming in his head. "I think I'll write him a note that says, 'I know how hard that must have been for you to write.' " Still chuckling, Hargadon moves on to the next of the more than 150 letters he will go through that day, a small fraction of the estimated 15,000 to 20,000 letters he will see over the course of the school year.

For Hargadon, any semblance of a sane work-pace disappeared with the last of the fall leaves. From early November, when he started reading the first of the early action applications, until early April, when he made up his mind about the last of the regular action candidates, he was flat-out, a man on a mission.

Not only would he arrive at the office before sunup to read

candidates' folders, but after other business of the day was done, he would be back reading folders by late afternoon, sometimes long into the night. Sometimes while reading, he paused to look at a map to locate a candidate's out-of-the-way home town. The more home towns he found, the better he felt, because they were proof that Princeton was attracting an increasingly diverse pool of applicants. At the start of the school year, he had made his usual resolution: Do not let the urgent preempt the important. As always, however, his schedule did him in.

In the year that I observed him, the dean personally read about two-thirds of the nearly 13,000 applications to Princeton. In between, he regularly devoured half a dozen newspapers and magazines, pausing sometimes to reflect on how what was going on in the outside world affected his own universe. One morning when he read in the *Times* that the birth rate goes down during the sort of recession the United States was currently in, his first thought was, "In twenty years, some dean of admission is going to have a tough problem." Usually when Hargadon's boss, Dean of the College Nancy Malkiel, showed him an interesting article she had clipped for him, Hargadon had already read it. When he finally got home around ten or eleven at night, he couldn't just fall into bed. "My mind is too much alive from the day to doze right off. I've got to"—what else?—"read myself tired."

On top of all this, it took the dean between an hour and a half to two hours a day just to read and sort his mail. To be sure, not every missive required Hargadon's personal attention. Many were just letters of recommendation that he could have put directly into the candidates' folders. But the dean always wanted to at least glance at what was addressed to him. Not only that, he wanted to personally reply, either with a letter or, in most cases, with an acknowledgment postcard that he would personally sign, often adding a handwritten postscript.

It was all very time-consuming, but to Hargadon it actually saved time. By acknowledging everything as it came in, he said, he headed off a lot of the letters and phone calls that would otherwise come in from people wanting to know whether their correspondence had been received. The dean could have used a signature machine rather than sign his name, but he knew that personalizing the process worked to his advantage in that, the more personal and caring the process appeared to be, the less anger toward Princeton a rejected candidate, his school, and his community would feel—all of which made it more likely that the next great student from that school would apply to Princeton.

Because Hargadon tried to eyeball all his mail, applicants had a valuable opportunity to get his attention through letters of recommendation written on their behalf. In the greater scheme of things, a letter of recommendation is likely to be less important than the applicant's own work: her academic record, her projects, and what she writes on her application essay. The same thing is true at other prestigious institutions. Still, an elite university's admissions department obviously wouldn't ask for such letters if they weren't seen as serving some purpose.

The purpose they are meant to serve, but very often fail to, is the same basic purpose of the alumni interviewer's report, the guidance counselor's report, and the teachers' reports. The letter of recommendation is intended to shed light on the "real" applicant by sharing personal observations and anecdotes that bring the student to life as a unique individual. Instead, what an admissions department usually gets is what Pomona's Bruce Poch calls "platitudes."

As a result, the letter of recommendation is without a doubt the most underutilized weapon in an applicant's arsenal. Students can't pick their interviewers; nor can most pick the high schools they attend, and hence the guidance counselor and teachers they get. But every young person has the power to pick someone in his life who will write an effective letter of recommendation. Not one of the five students I followed ever mentioned the importance of having someone write a revealing, anecdote-filled letter on his or her behalf— the kind of letter that might help compensate for their problems with their guidance counselors and alumni interviewers. Teachers' and guidance counselors' reports, according to Vanderbilt's assistant admissions dean Terry Cowdrey, are of vastly uneven quality, so that no student can afford not to use the letter of recommendation effectively.

Indeed, any applicant to a selective university will improve his chances of acceptance if he chooses his letter-writer (or writers) carefully. The key, as Hargadon's instructions on the application indicate, is to have someone "who knows you well write on your behalf. That person may be, for instance, a brother or sister, a parent, a coach, a music instructor, an employer, or friend."

About halfway through the stack of letters, Hargadon came across two letters written by a set of twins, each one writing about the other. The one twin said of her sister that her problem was she thought she could cook food twice as fast by doubling the temperature of the oven. Hargadon roared and said he would write her a note that now he knew what he was doing wrong. The other twin wrote that on a trip abroad her sister had told strangers that they were separated at birth and had just run into each other. Laughing still, Hargadon said he would write back that he would never be able to read another of those "separated at birth" tabloid-newspaper stories without smiling.

When I asked how much of a boost the twins would get from their obviously revealing and appealing letters, Hargadon said, a bit noncommittally, "It will add to their folders." But then he said with a twinkle in his eye, "Just the way they wrote about each other tells me a little something"—a little something that he liked.

Another letter of recommendation that Hargadon glanced at that day that seemed to have the kind of information he was looking for came from a college English teacher who had tutored the applicant. The letter described in detail how the student's language skills had improved over the last eighteen months. Another revealing letter came from a coach, who described how the applicant had worked his butt off and how much he had improved over his high school career. Another, which the dean wouldn't have time to read right now but which intrigued him, was a four-page handwritten letter from the grandfather of a candidate. Still another that held promise was written by someone in the office of the dean of students at Harvard who had known the applicant in question since he was a young boy.

All told, Hargadon's mail that day included 138 letters of recommendation. Half an hour into his task, he remarked, "It's just crazy all the mail I get. The more personal you try to make things, the more work you make for yourself." After a short pause, however, he resumed his task; "All of them *might* be important. That's why I look at them."

By the time he finished, Hargadon had cast an eye on letters of recommendation written by every manner of person in a candidate's life, a number of whom should have been intimately familiar with the candidate, a number of whom should not have been. They included:

- sixteen fathers of candidates, including one in Mexico and another in China
- ten mothers of candidates
- eleven sisters of candidates, one of whom was a Princeton student, and nine brothers of candidates, two of whom were Princeton students
- five grandfathers of candidates
- two aunts, one uncle, and the wife of an uncle of candidates
- the cousin of a candidate who was also the parent of a Princeton graduate
- twenty-six Princeton alumni, all of whom were writing about candidates who *weren't* their sons or daughters; one was a university trustee who, Hargadon knew off the top of his head, had written previous letters on behalf of four other candidates
- two U.S. Senators, one of whom committed the faux pas of addressing his letter: "To Whom It May Concern"

- one U.S. Congressman
- the Indian ambassador to Germany
- the attorney general of Samoa
- four Princeton professors
- the presidents of two other colleges
- an admissions official of another college
- nine secondary school principals and headmasters
- four teachers, including one in Sri Lanka
- a state education department official
- the academic dean of an Alabama prep school and the director of admissions of a Hawaii parochial school
- a violin teacher, a drama teacher, a yearbook adviser, and a choral director
- a football coach and a swimming coach
- one priest, two pastors, three ministers, a church activities director, a scoutmaster, and a camp counselor
- a landlord
- four family friends, one self-described "lovely friend," and one candidate family's neighbor
- the president of a corporation
- three candidates' supervisors on their summer jobs

After he was finished reading the mail, Hargadon walked outside his office to see what his secretary had put in his tray for him. At the top of the stack was another letter, this one written by an old high school classmate of Hargadon's, whom he hadn't seen in years and years. The dean started reading, and as he did he muttered under his breath.

"What's that?" I asked.

He showed me the letter, which in essence asked Har-

gadon, for old times' sake, to show his child special consideration. "Can you believe it?" he said. While the dean momen-
tarily considered telling the writer to go fly a kite, an
acknowledgment card was sent instead—*sans* a handwritten
note.

CHAPTER □ 12

E arly on the second Sunday in December, just a day or two
after the letters had gone in the mail informing early
action candidates whether they had been accepted, rejected,
or deferred, Hargadon was sitting at his kitchen table, sipping
a cup of coffee and reading the newspaper. The telephone
rang.

"Hello?"

"I want to talk to you about my daughter," a woman said,
her voice cracking with emotion. "I want you to know that I
haven't slept all night." Then: "You've ruined my family's
Christmas!" Then: "I think I'm going to have a nervous
breakdown!"

The woman's daughter's letter had told her that she had
been deferred until spring. Hargadon's first reaction: "I've
really got to get an unlisted phone number."

But while a part of him was laughing at the preposterous-
ness of the call, another part was angry that the woman had
intruded on his one day of relative peace and quiet each week.
As the woman continued to rant about how devastating an
experience this was, the dean made up his mind that the

woman's daughter probably was still asleep, knew nothing about what her mother was up to, and would be horrified if she knew.

"I'm sorry," he finally said in his best bedside manner. "I don't have your daughter's folder in front of me." Then, lest the woman think her call had served a useful purpose, he served up some watery gruel: "We had a lot of good candidates. We couldn't take them all." Then politely but firmly, he said good-bye.

☐ ☐ ☐ ▮ ☐

For Josh, Sirrka, Lucy, and Mark, finding out whether they were in or out or would be in limbo for another four months was an equally gut-wrenching experience: Did they have what Princeton and Harvard wanted or not?

Josh, an outstanding academic prospect, had strengths in math and science that were well suited to his declared interest in being an engineering major. He had very little in the way of extracurricular activities, but he had written—in my opinion, at least—a very strong and appealing essay that showed he would be an active learner in the classroom, plus a willing participant in a community that lived, worked, and played together. While he wasn't the leader of his high school marching band, the fact that he was a musician indicated he could help meet a community need. Would it be enough?

When Josh came home from school, the letter from Princeton was waiting for him, and so was his mother. All earlier thoughts of putting the letter around his neck on a chain vanished as he looked into his mom's anxious eyes. He looked at the envelope and, after a second or two, took a deep breath and ripped it open.

"Yes!" it began.

With a loud gasp of relief and happiness, mother and son hugged.

▯ ▯ ▯ ▮ ▯

Mark was still at school when he heard from a friend that the letters were arriving. His first reaction was: "Did Charlotte get in to Harvard?"

"Yeah! She did!" his friend shouted, then disappeared into a classroom.

Charlotte was the school's designated superstar, a girl with near-perfect grades and test scores, plus national awards in science and foreign languages. As Mark took his seat for the next class, he nervously rubbed his hands and thought, Of course Charlotte was going to get in. I knew that all along. It's not going to make any difference on whether I get in.

Still, by the final bell, Mark couldn't shake his sense of foreboding. As he drove home, his hands were trembling on the steering wheel. Alone, he kept saying out loud, "You've been deferred, you've been deferred"—even as he silently prayed that Harvard had accepted him.

While Mark wasn't first in his class, he was very near the top. Moreover, his "magnet" school's reputation was as well known on the East Coast as it was on the West Coast. He was an excellent violinist and had received national recognition for his playing. Still, in terms of academic achievement, Mark couldn't come near a kid like Josh.

He burst through the front door and nearly ransacked the

living room before he spotted the letter on the kitchen table, where his mother had put it. His hands were shaking as he tore it open. Seemingly from out of nowhere, his mother appeared and tried to put a comforting arm around her son's shoulders. But Mark edged away. Without saying a word, he went upstairs to his room and closed the door. He put on a recording of the violin concerto in D minor by Aram Khachaturian. Then, in a trancelike state, he picked up his violin and played along with the music.

□ □ □ ▌ □

When the school bell rang at exactly 1:48 P.M., Lucy dashed out the door, hopped into her car, and drove the short distance to her home. She pulled into the driveway and nervously made her way around to the front of the house. Slowly she opened the mailbox and found the letter from Princeton, in with the circulars and the utility bills. She went inside, sat down, and opened every other piece of mail first. Then, finally, she took the letter from Princeton in her hands and slit open the top of the envelope.

Lucy was the valedictorian of a so-so high school who hadn't had the benefit of strong counseling, who had written an essay that just didn't work, and who hadn't been the beneficiary of an anecdote-filled alumni interviewer's report. While she was very accomplished in math, she did not want to be an engineer, thus missing the chance to benefit from the university's objective to raise the number of its female engineering majors.

Lucy had not been rejected outright, but like Mark, she had been deferred.

Teary-eyed, Lucy called her mother, who told her to look on the bright side: at least she was still in the running. Later on, she went out with her boyfriend and drowned her sorrows in a huge ice-cream sundae, knowing that she now faced four more months of agonizing waiting.

▯ ▯ ▯ ▌ ▯

Sirrka's letter didn't arrive the day the letters for other early action applicants from her high school arrived. She went to see her guidance counselor, and he telephoned the admissions office. Sirrka and her counselor sat in his office for what seemed like an eternity, waiting for a staffer to get on the line and give them an answer.

Sirrka's choice of essay topic reflected her special interest in Eastern Europe. Had she indicated on her application that she wanted to major in Slavic studies or some similar department, her unusual background might have made a bigger difference. Hargadon might have forwarded her application to that academic department for review, and Sirrka just might have turned out to be *the* best candidate in that area in the entire applicant pool. But given that she ultimately wanted to be a doctor, her essay was not enough to make her interest in her homeland, or her application, stand out.

After what seemed an interminable wait, one of the Princeton staffers came on the line and gave Sirrka's counselor the verdict. She had been deferred.

As Sirrka left the counselor's office she started to cry. Slowly she made her way to the school library, where she was scheduled to be that period. She was still teary-eyed when two friends of hers—both guys—came over to her table. When they found out what was wrong, they tried to cheer her up by sharing an orange with her. Sirrka managed a smile, but just barely.

In all, approximately 2,000 students had applied to Princeton early action, and about 600 had been accepted. Nearly all the rest had been deferred. There were now roughly 12,000 candidates vying for 1,400 remaining letters of acceptance, to be mailed out at the end of the regular action period in early April. The statistical odds against getting in had risen to roughly eleven to one.

CHAPTER ◻ 13

Nora Simeon was only half awake when she walked into her 8:00 A.M. class, but it didn't take her long to realize that the high level of noise and excitement had nothing to do with the approaching holidays.

Her friend, Corrine, flushed and breathless, had just come back from the principal's office, where she had taken a call from her mother.

"I'm in!" shrieked Corrine. "Dartmouth let me in!"

Nora looked around at the excited crowds of kids clustering around the half-dozen who already knew where they were going next fall. She gave Corrine a quick hug and a smile, then grabbed her seat and buried her head in her book.

Nora, the last of our five students, had not yet begun to fill out her applications.

Nora is a thin-boned girl with short black hair and thick horn-rimmed glasses. Physically underdeveloped, she dresses older than her age—pleated skirts or tailored slacks with a button-down shirt and brightly colored sweater. Her skin is porcelain like her mother's. Her clipped speech and precise physical mannerisms—some reminiscent of a marine drill instructor—come from her father.

Nora lives with her father, mother, and two younger brothers in a majestic two-story, center-hall Colonial in an ultra-exclusive community not far from Philadelphia. Theirs is a grand, distinctive home, with antique maple and walnut tables, wing chairs, and deep-cushion sofas. The thirty-foot-long living room is tastefully decorated with Persian rugs, Oriental vases, and European oil paintings.

In the Simeons' community—Upper Roselle, Pennsylvania—the average household income is over $150,000 a year. Sunday afternoons find casually chic-looking parents rooting for their kids' soccer teams. The parking lots at the train station contain an opulent mix of Beemers, Benzes, and four-wheel-drive utility vehicles, many of the latter an Eddie Bauer green with tan trim.

Upper Roselle's 30,000 residents are a mixture of upwardly mobile executives (both male and female), professors and administrators at nearby colleges and universities, artists and writers, plus a smattering of the horsey set who still fox-hunt. But while vocations and avocations in Upper Roselle vary only slightly, the ethnic mix varies even less.

As his first name suggests, Nora's father—Ahmed—is not like his neighbors. Born in Lebanon, he attended private school in England, receiving his undergraduate degree from Cambridge. He crossed the Atlantic to get a master's degree in business administration from Harvard and went on to a distinguished career in international finance, specializing in the Middle East. His wife, Saria, is Malaysian, making their children an even more exotic mix. Saria has a degree from a university in Singapore.

Nora's public high school is acknowledged to be one of the best secondary schools—public or private—in the United

States. While other schools, even very good ones, are lucky if they get one or two kids into Harvard, Princeton, and Yale every two or three years, Upper Roselle High School has a tradition of sending a dozen or more kids a year to just those three, and a quarter of the senior class to other highly selective colleges or universities. Though Nora has never been first in her class, she has never ranked lower than third.

▯ ▯ ▯ ▮ ▯

A few days before Nora's senior year began, she and her mother visited colleges in New England. It was one of those if-it's-Tuesday-this-must-be-Belgium trips, and Nora and Saria set foot on ten campuses in seventy-two hours. Harvard, Yale, and Brown were among the destinations, as were a couple of women's colleges and Amherst, a small, liberal-arts college that Nora had never heard of, which Saria added to the list at the last minute because they were going to be in the area.

It was raining when they got to Providence, Rhode Island, and Brown, to Nora's way of thinking, could best be described as "run-down." Based on nothing more than this superficial impression and despite Brown's outstanding reputation, Nora decided on the spot not to apply. And thus she made what Hargadon says is one of the biggest mistakes a young person can make in choosing a college, namely: not thinking enough about what one wants out of the experience other than the degree, then applying to the ones that seem the best "match."

Except for Josh, all my kids were susceptible to making the same naïve mistake. Lucy had initially made Harvard her top choice after looking at magazine rankings. Mark had applied to Harvard partly because his older brother had gone there, and he felt he was expected to as well. Sirrka had simply fallen in love with the look of the Princeton campus. Only Josh was in tune with Hargadon's advice to look for the best match, which was ironic because during his first three years of high school, he seemed to be the only student in his class who didn't know exactly where he wanted to go. But while the others had been parroting ideas foisted on them by their parents, Josh's parents had been smart enough to let him make up his own mind. When he finally decided that he wanted to go to a university that had both a strong engineering school and a strong liberal arts program, he made Princeton and Stanford his first and second choice, dropping a not-too-shabby place called the Massachusetts Institute of Technology down to third.

Finding the right match also means looking past how people commonly perceive a college. B. Ann Wright, dean of enrollment management at Smith College, says that when many parents think of a women's college like Smith they believe, "We will protect their daughter with high walls from the real world." But those who delve into Smith's real personality, Wright says, find the opposite: a very politically active school.

"Every school," says Vanderbilt's dean of undergraduate admissions, Neill F. Sanders, "has its own personality."

That fall, Nora and her father argued several times at the dinner table over whether Nora should apply to Harvard. Having gone to graduate school there, Dad couldn't understand why Nora didn't appreciate what he was telling her about the wide variety of courses and activities at his alma mater. Nora ended one argument by loudly proclaiming that Harvard simply wasn't for her and that was that.

When I asked Nora why Harvard wasn't for her, she said it was too big and had an "ugly" campus located in the middle of a city.

She didn't sound like she meant it, however, so I pressed her. Eventually she confessed that she would love to go to Harvard but couldn't apply because if she was rejected she would hate herself for disappointing her father.

Nora agreed to apply to Yale because a friend of the family really wanted her to, and she felt it would be insulting to her friend and even to her parents if she didn't. Even if she were to get into Yale, however, she didn't want to go there—not that the Yale admissions department was going to know that when it read her application.

Nora wasn't alone in the pressure she felt to climb the Ivy. In January I led a discussion with several high school seniors organized by a guidance counselor in an affluent suburban community. One of the kids around the table, a good-looking young man, said that when he had told his friends he was applying to prestigious but non-Ivy Duke, they had screwed up their faces and looked at him as if he were nuts. A dark-haired girl said that when she was an underclassman, she had vowed not to apply to either Harvard or Yale because she didn't think she would be happy at a big school, no matter how good it was. But then her father had started talking to her about her college plans, as had friends of the family. "The only place anyone in this town wants you to go to is Harvard, Yale, or Princeton," she complained. "My values have been thrown totally out of whack," she added. "I now place more value on the name of a school than on what it has to offer. I feel like a total snob." The others, however, said she was right to "go Ivy." Echoing Tom Masters, the father I had met on the tour of the Princeton campus, one of the kids said, "People judge you by the college you went to."

Nora had wound up making Princeton her first choice for both the wrong reason and the right reason. The wrong reason was Princeton's "prestige." The right reason was that Nora had friends at Princeton with whom she had spent time—she had slept in a dormitory, eaten with undergraduates, and gone to selected classes—and she had loved the environment. Yale was going to be her second choice, followed by two small liberal arts colleges, including the one her mother had added to the New England itinerary at the last minute. Nora had really liked Amherst. Indeed, she had liked it so much that after the campus tour ended, she had talked at great length with her tour guide, who had filled her in on courses, the library, dorm life, campus activities, and all the other things that figure in matching a college to a student. I had the distinct feeling that while Nora's head said go to Princeton, her heart said go to this smaller college with the slightly less glossy reputation.

Nora had planned to start filling out her college applications in September. She had even marked it down on her calendar. But as September, then October and November, went by the boards, there had always been something else that got in her way. Little wonder. Nora was taking advanced-placement English, calculus, European history, and French, plus physics and Spanish. She was co-chair of her school's environmental club, head of its science club, head of the school literary magazine, and publicity manager of the school orchestra, in which she played the violin. On top of all that, she was in her fourth year of learning Japanese on her own time, having gone to Tokyo the last two weeks of her summer vacation, just before the whirlwind college tour and just after a six-week course in calculus, which she felt she had to take if she were to do well in her senior AP calculus class. She also was spending one afternoon a week as a hospital volunteer.

I estimated that Nora was probably an academic two. Overloaded as she was and always tired, she had managed to score around or above 700 on all her college boards. She had managed to be ranked in the top one percent of her very-competitive high school class. In Nora, Hargadon was going to see a candidate who clearly had an extremely high energy level, and who he could count on to participate in many of the activities that make a university community vibrant. He was going to see a young woman who had intellectual curiosity and who was intrinsically, not extrinsically, motivated. "There are so many other things I still want to try," she told me out of the blue one day.

As for her extracurricular activities in high school, Nora was probably a three. While she was used to a heavy work-load, she hadn't foreseen all the extra work she would have to do when other officers were kicked out of the environmental club because they weren't doing their jobs. It became Nora's responsibility to arrange for the floats her club was making for a fall festival. On a Saturday in November it also fell to her to set up a booth in town for passersby to sign postcards to be mailed to the White House urging the President to better protect the environment.

This was her passion. On the walls of her bedroom she had posters of endangered species. That day, nobody walked by without Nora trying to thrust a ballpoint pen into their hands. "We *have* to protect the environment!" she kept saying.

While some people were put off, a large number were caught up in her eco-evangelism. Dozens signed on the dotted line.

"This sounds really corny," she said later, "but I really felt like I made a difference today."

Nora had had her mettle tested. Not only had she held the environmental club together, she had changed the format of its newsletter and gotten more kids both to read it and write for it. She had organized other kids to pressure the school administration to buy recycled paper, and she had even held money-raising promotions to help the school defray recycled paper's extra cost. That fall, under Nora's leadership, the environmental club had polled local gas stations to see if they were conforming with clean-air regulations.

To be sure, in Nora, Hargadon wasn't going to see one of *the* best students in America in any particular academic subject, or athletic or musical talent. Still, Nora's trump card, it seemed to me, was the outstanding academic record she achieved at a high school whose reputation was certain to be noted on the readers' cards. What top colleges want most in a student is academic achievement and motivation.

☐ ☐ ☐ ❙ ☐

It was December 27 when Nora finally realized she was running out of tomorrows. The chances of her writing an application that was going to bring out all of her strengths were slim to none by now. James W. Wickenden, a former Princeton admissions head who runs his own educational consulting firm, emphasizes in his firm's college-counseling handbook that the applicant's goal "should be to create a coherent, well thought out application that sheds light on all the important aspects of your character. A mad dash to the finish line is unlikely to achieve that result."

Even students who apply early to one college often hurt themselves by waiting until the last minute to fill out five or six other applications. Many students get lulled into thinking they don't have to do anything else until they hear from their early action schools, so that when the letters come the first week of December saying, as most do, that the applicant has been deferred, students must make a mad dash to finish their other applications on time. It had happened to Mark Ghani when Harvard deferred him. During the focus-group discussion that I had with high school seniors, one of them said he had written eight essays in four days. When I asked whether he thought any of them were good, he said, "Not as good as they could have been."

Nora's applications reflected her procrastination. For one college, she wrote an essay describing her work with the environmental club; for another, she tacked on a new introductory paragraph, turning it into an essay on "values." The transformation was transparent, as the recycled essay began: "Two values I hold—those of dedication and being practical—are reflected in the piece below."

It didn't help matters that Nora filled out her applications while she was suffering from a bad cold. For three days straight, she sat at her desk in her bathrobe, hacking and sneezing as she wrote. From time to time, she went down-stairs to the kitchen and swilled from a carton of orange juice. Then she willed herself back to her desk and waited until her head had cleared enough to continue writing.

By the end of the third day, Nora's parents were equally exhausted. Ahmed slowly typed his daughter's essays on the computer in the den, constantly checking and rechecking, over the rim of his eyeglasses, for spelling errors. Then he laid out the envelopes for the applications and was so wiped out that he double- and triple-checked each envelope before licking it shut. Saria kept rubbing Nora's shoulders and brewing pots of very black coffee that her daughter gulped down. Then, after almost literally carrying Nora to bed and tucking her in, Saria sped to the post office and made sure the word *overnight* was stamped on each envelope.

Of the several applications Nora banged out over that seventy-two-hour period, only Princeton's made a strong personal impression on her, mostly because of Hargadon's hodge-podge questions, which she found fun to answer despite her mental and physical exhaustion. For her favorite book, she put *Lord of the Rings*. For her favorite time of day, she wrote twilight. For her favorite section of the newspaper, she put the comics section. For her favorite quote, she wrote: "Your final destination is not the important point; it's the journey that matters."

While these were certainly not bad answers, it was hard to see any of them reaching Hargadon. Had Nora allowed herself more time, she might have chosen to use another quote that she had used in an essay for another college that probably was a better window into her individuality. The quote was from Supreme Court Justice Benjamin Cardozo. She would leave high school, Nora wrote, "not merely with knowledge of the subjects I have studied, but hopefully knowing that I have made a difference, perhaps a small one, but *'The difference is no less real because of its degree.'* "

Neither did Nora's Princeton application reflect that she was a particularly active learner. Instead of writing about the environmental club, Nora told Princeton that her "greatest satisfaction" lay in studying several foreign languages.

"My interest in foreign languages has led me to learn four of them. I began studying at the . . . language school after we served as hosts to a family from [Japan] four years ago. I had an opportunity to go to Japan on scholarship last summer [with two classmates] where we stayed with host families. While I was concerned with my ability to communicate, I was also nervous about my capacity to adapt to their lifestyles. While the families made us feel at home, I played my part in that adjustment. I found that I integrated smoothly, and, albeit with the help of a dictionary, communicated in halting and jumbled Japanese, without shyness. I returned to the United States, satisfied that I had successfully overcome my initial concerns."

Even during the mad rush at the end of December, Nora might have benefited from the help of a counselor like Nancy Siegel or Edith Warnock, both of whom likely would have suggested that instead of trying to write a bunch of new essays, she should use some polished compositions she had previously written in class. Indeed, Warnock had done exactly that with one of her clients—over the objections of the kid's parents, who felt that their son ought to write something "momentous" that would "impress" the likes of Hargadon.

To be sure, applying to college is something students should take the lead on, as Hargadon says, thereby demonstrating their independence and initiative. As such, it may be as wrong for counselors to dominate the kids as it is for parents. But the fact remains that Nora's counselor had more than two hundred other students to keep track of. Weeks after the January 1 filing deadline passed, when he found out that Nora had waited until the very last minute to do her applications, he said, "I'd have been pulling my hair out if I had known what was going on."

Good counseling might also have helped Nora put her "wrong" as well as her right foot forward, as Hargadon advises. Asked to describe the "biggest mistake" she ever made, Nora wrote: "Although I have made many mistakes in my life, there are few large enough to merit description in a college application. The mistake I most regret is that I never put in the time or effort necessary for practice to become a really good violinist, which I am told I could be. As it is never too late, I have begun practicing more seriously. I am happy to have gained enjoyment from and insight into music through my study of the violin."

Nice sentiments, certainly, but clearly not the sort of response Hargadon was looking for. After the school year was over, Hargadon told Stanford's admissions head, James Montoya that he had asked some of the applicants what the toughest part of the application was. They said it was the question about the biggest mistake. Students were worried about what was the "right" big mistake to have made. Montoya also reported in Stanford's alumni magazine that Hargadon had said, "The funniest answer we got was from a young woman. She said, 'I dated John Jones,' or whatever his name was. And, 'What did you learn from it?' 'Don't ever date guys with shaved heads.' She clearly approached that question head on."

Nora's application just didn't do her justice.

CHAPTER ☐ **14**

One day in January, Millburn's guidance counselor Nancy Siegel made the mistake of opening her refrigerator door. Staring at the empty shelves, she knew she couldn't put it off any longer.

Going to the supermarket might not sound like a big deal, but this wasn't a good time of year for Siegel to walk down the aisles by herself. She told her teenage daughter to put on a coat and get in the car.

As Mom pushed the grocery cart, Daughter ran interference, allowing Siegel to shop without having to stop every other minute to answer the question on the mind of most of the Millburn seniors' parents: Do you think my child will get in?

If Siegel's daughter weren't around to ride shotgun, Siegel might as well have hung a sign on the front of her cart that said "The doctor is in." "We always have to be aware of what we look like and the expressions on our faces. We have to smile and say, 'Oh, yes, how did the interview go?' We have to remember everybody's name. We end up becoming the repositories of their anxieties," says Siegel's colleague, Ellen

Brener, adding that if she had it to do over, she would never live in the community where she worked.

While the counselors do their best to reassure the parents, on their own they worry just as much. For just as parents have no way of knowing who else is in a university's applicant pool, the only thing guidance counselors have to go on is how other kids from their school have fared over the years. "The process is too secretive," says Siegel. "Who are these colleges answerable to? No one!"

This January, having no way to judge how things were going to turn out, the only thing Siegel and Brener could do was sit and wait until April. Well, not exactly sit. Throughout the fall and winter, up until the first flowers of spring, the Millburn High School guidance office was spinning like a top.

Siegel and company each had fifty or more nail-biting seniors whom they were shepherding through the admissions process. Each had more than 150 other advisees, including special-education students, who require a lot of individual attention. On top of all this the counselors were constantly dealing with such social problems as the effects of divorce, and they were working with girls and boys to prevent unwed pregnancies.

Every day seemed to produce a new crisis. Sometimes the problem required the sleuthing abilities of Sherlock Holmes. One day Siegel got a phone call from someone in the Harvard admissions office. It was probably the most mysterious phone call she has ever gotten in her twenty-five years as a high school guidance counselor. The caller wanted Siegel's help with a particular student who was applying to Harvard and about whom something unflattering had been written. When

Siegel asked who had written the essay or report that was problematic, the Harvard person said he couldn't get into that without breaching the confidentiality of the admissions process. When Siegel asked how she was supposed to help if she didn't know what the problem was or who was responsible for it, the Harvard person offered no suggestions.

Siegel hung up, then stood and looked out the window at the football field and the line of tall trees beyond. In her mind, she eliminated possible suspects. Whatever was troubling Harvard, she knew it wasn't something she herself had written. Neither was it something in the student's application, because she had read the application before the student sent it in. Nor had it been something the principal had written, because she had read that, too. If the problem involved the alumni interviewer's report, Harvard would not be calling her. Most likely, she surmised, it was something that one of the two teachers had written in their reports. She didn't want to be too intrusive, so she asked each teacher whether they had written anything that could be "misinterpreted" by Harvard. Just in case, she said to each of them, would you please write another letter? They did.

The counselors saw some of their college-frantic seniors once a day, every day, for weeks on end. One day a girl came into Siegel's office with tears in her eyes. "My mother insists that I apply to this college," she said, "but I don't want to go there. I want to go to this other college. What should I do?" On the side of the student but not wanting to anger the mother, who might complain to the principal or the school board, Siegel wrote down a list of reasons why she agreed with the girl that the college she wanted to go to would be a better match for her. The girl thanked her, and as she got up to leave, Siegel added, "You know you're still going to have to apply to the school your mother wants you to go to, don't you?" The girl sighed and nodded.

Siegel didn't know which Millburn students would get into which elite universities, but she understood the importance prestigious institutions place on students being independent and doing their own applications. Just before Christmas break, a boy came into her office with fire in his eyes. At first Siegel thought she was on the hot seat, but that space was reserved for the boy's mom and dad. He unequivocally declared, "I will not show my parents this essay because I know this isn't what they want me to write." The boy waited, expecting Siegel to object. "Fine," she replied softly, "let's see what you've got." The essay went in as it was.

Sometimes Siegel found herself refereeing parent-child disagreements over applications. One day another boy brought his mother in to see Siegel. Siegel, at the boy's request, read his college essay aloud. When she was finished, she looked the mother in the eye and said, "Who wrote this?" Flustered, the mother replied that she might have sharpened a phrase or two. "This isn't the boy I know," Siegel said to her advisee, who then turned to his mother and said, "I told you so." Siegel quickly calmed things down and told the boy to write his own essay.

In all these months, meanwhile, the phone never stopped ringing. One Monday morning a mother called with the latest "hot" rumor, which Siegel figured had gotten started the way most of them do—at a cocktail party in town. The rumor was that Harvard, Princeton, and Yale had all agreed to take only half as many Millburn students as they had the year before. "Is it true?" this mother wanted desperately to know. Siegel tried not to laugh, but she couldn't contain herself. "Of course not," she said. After hanging up, she threw up her arms and said, "The rumors get crazier every year."

Another day a college admissions person from a western university called Brener to say, "I don't like something I hear" in one student's essay. The essay, the admissions person explained, made the girl sound like a loner. Brener said the girl was a solitary sort but reassured the caller that based on her knowledge of her, she would reach out to more people as she matured. The caller seemed satisfied, though once again Brener knew it was going to be a long wait until April.

Another counselor, Charles Yeamans, got a call from a woman whose husband was being transferred to New York. She said they were thinking of buying a house in Millburn but that, before they made up their minds, they were checking on the average SAT scores for several high schools in the area.

Even though the counselors tell students and their parents that SATs are not the end-all and be-all of the college admissions process, everyone was still preoccupied with them. "We tell the kids not to bother taking the SAT prep courses but to spend their time doing something else they're good at," says Brener, adding, "It doesn't matter. They all take the courses anyway." When one junior told Brener that her SAT tutor had told her to take the tests in the fall of her junior year, immediately after completing the prep course, Brener went ballistic. She wanted the name of that tutor so she could scold him. Recommending that the girl take the tests so early, she and Siegel felt, was self-serving on the tutor's part. If the girl didn't get great scores, which she likely would not, the tutor would sign her up for more tutoring. Brener told the girl: "I don't want to see you take more than two sets of SATs, and if you're going to take the first one in November of your junior year, when the heck are you going to take the second one?"

Brener's pique extended to some of the colleges themselves. One college wanted its applicants to write an essay about what they liked the most or the least about their community. "That just infuriates me!" she steamed. "The kids don't know enough to be able to answer that one. They're coming to me asking, 'What am I supposed to say?' "

Siegel was upset, too, the day one of her freshman advisees said hello to her and she didn't even know the student's name. If only we had one more counselor, she thought.

To be sure, the counselors did know some ninth graders, but that was only because special problems brought certain students to the office. Siegel, a twenty-five-year veteran at Millburn, was worried that she wasn't laying the proper groundwork for the freshmen so that, by the time they were juniors, they would see the guidance office as a resource. She had proposed to the higher-ups that shortly before midterm exams, freshmen come into the guidance office in small groups so that they could ease their jitters by chatting with sophomores. The idea was nixed because the group sessions weren't deemed important enough to justify frosh losing twenty to twenty-five minutes of class time.

░ ░ ░ ▮ ░

On the surface, the free-flowing approach that Siegel and company used seemed to make an already-chaotic situation worse. On some days as many as fifty students would all be talking in the office at once, driving even Siegel to distraction. After a while, however, it became clear that the guidance office was an oasis for the students. It was a place where they could go during their study period, lunch period, or before or after school. They treated the place like the library, except that talking was not only allowed but encouraged. The teenagers would sit in small groups and talk about whatever was on their minds—their classes, or the kid who got fall-down drunk at the party on Saturday night. Brener, Siegel, and the others were just there—listening, observing, and soaking up impressions. They were learning about the young people, while at the same time the teenagers were learning about and from one another.

When it came time for the counselors to write letters of recommendation for the students, they were able to make use of the personal impressions they had soaked up. Using language that might have come out of Hargadon's own mouth, Brener said, "We can tell a college about a young person's character, values, how he or she approaches problems, how he or she reaches out to others. We can tell a college who the citizens are going to be in their community."

For the students themselves, the free-for-all atmosphere in the office provided a unique learning opportunity. They felt no pressure to know the "right" answer or to be anything but themselves. As a result, the guidance office came close to being the kind of open-ended high school classroom that a top university likes to see.

A couple of the discussions were sustained over several weeks and involved as many as forty different students. One particularly meaty give-and-take grew out of a debate raging in town over whether holiday decorations should be allowed in the public schools. Jewish and Christian students had different perspectives, but not always the perspective one would have expected: Some of the Christian students felt it was wrong to impose their religion on others, while some of the Jewish students felt that decorations were okay because religion had played such an important role in the founding of America. The latter point of view prompted a discussion of how Congress and the courts have approached the issue of separation of church and state down through the years.

One minute personal, the next scholarly, in these discussions the young people were learning on three different levels at once—each level one that a selective university wants students to have thoroughly explored. First, they were engaged in academic learning on a variety of subjects, including history, government, law, and religion. Second, they were learning about themselves in a natural, nonthreatening way— which would make it a little bit easier for them to be themselves when it came time to apply to college. Third, they were learning how to get along in a community of different-thinking people.

From the point of view of a university, such discussions are more productive when the student body is more ethnically and culturally diverse than that of nearly all-white Millburn. Pomona's Bruce Poch says the applicants he found "really appealing" were those from very diverse high schools, who just naturally had learned how to "communicate with kids very unlike themselves."

Still, the Socratic-style discussions in the Millburn guidance office were exactly the sort that veteran Princeton history professor Michael Mahoney had in mind when he spoke at a seminar on "What Kind of Student Does Princeton Want?" The "best kind of class," Mahoney said, is the one in which the teacher can leave the room and the discussion will continue uninterrupted.

If Millburn's guidance office teemed with inquisitive students, it wasn't by chance. Like a snake-charmer, Siegel drew students in by, among other things, keeping a jar of candy on her desk. When a youngster said he had just come in for the candy, Siegel would size up the expression on his face. If it wasn't his usual expression, she would shoo the other kids out of her office—or wait until she ran into him later in a hallway, in front of his locker, or anywhere else—then quietly ask him if something was wrong. Bouncing from one student to the next, Siegel's office was often still full an hour after school. Sometimes she had to call her own teenage son at home to tell him he would have to find another ride to whatever activity he had that afternoon.

But Siegel's efforts even went beyond her office.

One of her advisees, rather like Josh Hastings, was an absolute whiz in math. Indeed, the girl was going to finish the most difficult math course in her high school before her senior year. But while Josh's counselor hadn't had a clue as to what course Josh should take next, Siegel knew exactly what she wanted for her student.

First, she talked to the chair of Millburn's math department about her initiative and got him to support it. Then, together, they got in touch with the head of the Princeton math department and asked if it would be possible for Princeton to devise a special course for their student. The Princeton math chair invited them to drive down for the day. While Siegel walked around observing the math classrooms, the girl, the chair of the Millburn math department, and the chair of the Princeton math department worked out a senior-year curriculum for her that combined elements of three different undergraduate courses offered by the university.

So while it had taken a mother's determination to keep Josh challenged in math, this girl got the chance to become a superstar college candidate, thanks to the counseling services that every high school in America should be providing its brightest students, but that few do.

CHAPTER □ 15

Even compared with the overworked counselors at Millburn High School, Mark Ghani was having a lousy winter.

It was five forty-five on a Wednesday morning, and Mark was swatting wildly at the snooze-control button on his alarm clock. He hit it once, then twice more over the next twenty minutes. Then suddenly he realized that he was late for school. He crawled out of bed, dragged himself over to his dresser, and tried to pick out something to wear. He couldn't decide, so he put on the pants he had worn the day before and went downstairs to the kitchen. His parents were still asleep, so there was no danger of being yelled at for skipping breakfast. He rummaged through the corner pantry until he found a bagel, then clamped it between his teeth, slung his backpack over his shoulder, and took his car keys from a hook near the back door. As always, getting to school on time was going to take some doing.

With reading to do and papers to write for his regular homework, Mark was in a daze most of the time, including while he was driving. That was why he didn't see the car stopped at the traffic light in front of him. At the last second, he slammed on the brakes, but it was too late. He rear-ended the guy but good. Fortunately, no one was seriously hurt.

Then, just before Christmas, Mark's school orchestra gave a concert. As first violinist, Mark had the responsibility of tuning the orchestra before the concert, and he also was on the program as a featured soloist.

But as the orchestra members took their seats, the first violinist's chair remained empty. When it came time to tune the orchestra, the chair was still empty. When it came time for Mark to perform his solo, he was nowhere in the house. The next morning Mark's friend called him on the telephone. "Where were you last night?"

"I was here at home, finishing my applications."

Mark, now a zombie, had forgotten all about the concert.

Every day Mark would come home from school, go up to his room, and start his homework. Then he would put his head down on his desk and fall asleep until his mother called him for dinner. After dinner, he would do more homework until midnight. Then he would get up at six and start all over again. It was a treadmill: doing schoolwork Monday through Thursday, college applications all day Saturday and Sunday, then back to homework Sunday night. The pace actually accelerated when Harvard deferred him. Suddenly he had eight applications to complete.

At first, he would just stare at the applications, overwhelmed by the sheer amount of work involved.

From time to time, Mark's extended family would get together. By December, the relatives were worried. One Sunday afternoon, Mark's uncle took him aside and told him to try and relax. But then the uncle made the mistake of asking Mark what he wanted to study in college. "I can't think about that!" Mark shouted.

As Mark ground out his applications, his father didn't put any extra pressure on him, but his mother did.

Since his essay about how he so wanted to go to Harvard had gotten him only a deferral, Mark's mother suggested that he write his Princeton essay about an experience at the hospital where he was a volunteer. Mark resisted, arguing that the experience "didn't mean anything to me." (It was because Sirrka's experience with hospital work had meant so much to her that she *should* have written about it.) Mark wanted to write something "original."

Later that night, he went up to the study where the family computer was, locked the door, and put on the same piece by Khachaturian that he had listened to after getting his deferral letter from Harvard. He wanted to keep listening to the music much more than write this last essay. But soon enough he was tapping at the keyboard.

He wrote a crazy-sounding story about a young man who, while trying to find his college application, runs into two characters from his favorite book who are talking about him. They chat for a while, then the young man hears some classical music. The young man goes on to describe the music, its obscure composer, and the pleasure he feels when listening to music, compared with the angst he feels right now because he doesn't know what to say in this essay.

My eyes went blurry and the translated prose of *The Odyssey* began to disappear in splotches. I laid the spine up on my pillow and rubbed my eyelids. It was time. From a little white room doused with white light, the Princeton application lying on the computer keyboard screamed a piercing scream that made my temples tighten.... I staggered blindly into the half-light of the hallway, and as I regained my vision I heard the voices of the sirens. They lured me sweetly and rhythmically from down the hall, singing the tranquil "Andante Sostenuto" from the Khachaturian Violin Concerto. They tried to trick me with tantalizing offers to take away my fatigue and write my essay. Jerking away, I shook their spell, suddenly realizing that their song was a trick to divert my attentions from the mission at hand. As I bounded down the stairs to meet my papery fate I plowed into Mathieu from *The Age of Reason* and Mearsault from *A Happy Death*. (Undoubtedly they were discussing me.) Once they had picked themselves up off the landing, I asked their opinions on the essay topic. "The writing must come from your lust to get into college," Mathieu announced confidently. "And the more radical the better."

"Don't try to run away from it," Mearsault coolly confided. "Unless you write about something close to your heart, your essay will never work." He looked at Mathieu with an air of smug correctness. They continued up the stairs discussing my latest violin audition failure. Suddenly, my eyelids began to flutter, and a strong wind blew my hair in all different directions. Then lightning struck. "I'll write my essay about music. If I can capture my love of music and slap it, still breathing on the page, then the admissions officer will really know me!" ... I was downstairs at the computer in an instant, and I started to write:

"The violin has taught me discipline and responsibility. It

has given me something to be passionate about, and another definition of beauty. As a six-year-old child, I didn't realize that starting the violin would have such an impact on the way I thought. Now I am grateful that music is a prominent part of my life."

I had barely heaved a sigh of relief when Gregor Samsa from "Metamorphosis" scuttled under the door. He motioned toward the essay and shrugged seven of his shoulders. "You should have waited for my help," his eyes seemed to say. Pretending not to notice him, I snatched up the application and left the room.

Unlike his Harvard essay, Mark didn't slave over his essay for Princeton. Indeed, the first draft was also the final draft. When he finished at around two in the morning, he stuck the essay under his parents' door and went to bed. He was certain they were going to think it was ridiculous, but to his surprise, they liked its style. "It's certainly you," his mother said. She wanted him to change the name of the composer, but Mark refused, and so the essay went in exactly as the uninhibited Mark had written it.

Unlike her previous effort for Princeton, Lucy's essay for Duke was far more uninhibited. The assignment was to write about the person you would like most to interview if you had the chance.

Like Mark, Lucy wrote her more expressive essay late at night, feeling very deflated because she had been deferred by her first-choice school. Like Mark, she really just wanted to get the damned thing over with. As a result, she wrote straight from the heart, without trying to tailor her essay to fit any preconceived notion of what Duke wanted to read.

... The person that I would most like to interview is Sammy (Sammy Bull) Gravano. For the uninitiated, Sammy Bull is a co-defendant and consigliere (counselor) of John (The Teflon Don) Gotti, the alleged leader of the New York faction of the Gambino Crime Family. Sammy Bull has recently made the news by agreeing to testify for the United States Government against Gotti, his former boss and closest friend, in its case against Gotti in which he is charged with, amongst other crimes, murder.

... Why (interview) an alleged mobster? ... This is not simply a case of just another mobster looking to save his own crooked hide at the expense of one that he has taken a blood oath with; this situation is a clear example of what is wrong with society.

Although I'm not advocating any type of criminal activity, I am deeply disturbed at the ease with which "men of honor" can break their blood oaths. These men, whose honor supposedly means everything to them, who in the past would rather go to jail than to answer questions from a prosecutor, are becoming increasingly more likely to turn in their comrades in order to increase their own positions.

This trend merely mirrors society's own increasing selfishness. People are no longer interested in helping the less fortunate of society; this is evidenced by the decrease in government spending on social programs and education. . . .

It appears that people join the Mob today for the same reasons they once joined IBM. Good job, decent pay, some nice extras with the job. Nothing more. . . .

The Mafia is a family organization (however illegal its goals) which has lasted for generations due to its ever-loyal employees. In these selfish times, we could always depend

on the existence of death, taxes and the Mafia. Not anymore.

Lucy's essay succeeds in revealing her offbeat sense of
humor, as well as her concern for social problems. Like Josh's
car accident *cum* physics lesson and Mark's literary escapade,
it works emotionally as well as intellectually.

CHAPTER □ **16**

When the first of January drew nigh, a few thousand last-minute applications (including Mark's and Nora's) flooded into the Princeton admissions office; all of them had to be sorted, read, commented on, and decided upon by early April. Throughout January and February, the folders piled up, filling up the old couch in Hargadon's office and much of the floor around his desk. The stack of unanswered mail was nearly a foot high. It was time to reach for the office's monster bottle of vitamin C.

The new staffers hadn't read any of the two thousand or so applications of the early action period. They had been busy visiting high schools all over the United States and conducting the group "information" sessions for applicants visiting the Princeton campus. Now, however, every pair of eyes was needed, which meant that Hargadon conducted some last-minute training sessions for new members of his team. Then the monastery was sealed to the outside world.

Even though he was reading and training around the clock, however, Hargadon still attended meetings out of the office, including administrative meetings and disciplinary committee meetings. He had to write memos and otherwise advise Harold T. Shapiro, the university president, and other university officials on a variety of admissions-related subjects. The dean was also busy sending out the university's new video, *Conversations That Matter,* with the Zen-like opening line: "What difference in the universe is our moment of consciousness?" Copies were going out to applicants who had already been accepted as a way of encouraging them to say yes to Princeton (and no, in many cases, to Harvard and/or Yale). One admittee who got the video had a sister at Princeton who was in the video. Hargadon wrote at the bottom of the letter that accompanied her copy: "I suspect you've probably seen this video more than you want to by now." He also drew a circle with a smile.

At any time of day, Hargadon scribbled notes to himself about things to follow up on. One day he cut a story out of *USA Today* about a high school in a small town in Arkansas. Using parents to augment the teachers' roles, this school had been able to turn out a number of exceptionally-qualified college candidates. "It shows that a place with few resources can still do a good job," Hargadon said optimistically. Then he wrote a note to himself to check whether Princeton had any candidates from this school.

By early winter, the gray, windswept skies caused both Princeton students and the people who select them to go a little crazy. What the admissions department did went unnoticed, but the students' annual escapade attracted national attention. Unlike the students, Hargadon and his staff kept their clothes on.

As dictated by tradition, the students' escapade took place

the night of the first snowfall of the season. More than one hundred undergraduates gathered in a courtyard, many of them wearing masks, sneakers, and nothing in between. With an Olympic-style torchbearer leading the way, they took off at a signal and ran around the campus, screaming as they went. While most of the crazed were men, enough women were mixed in to cause local paparazzi to click away, once again recording for posterity what has become known as the Nude Olympics.

The skies were clear, but the air no less biting, the night Hargadon called a time-out and herded everyone out in front of West College. As the staff stretched their legs, the dean told them how lucky they all were to be working nonstop through the weekend. This being a Friday night, his comment went over like a lead balloon. "No, really," he said, deadpanning all the way. "Here we could be at home, worrying about how we are going to spend our weekend off. We're so lucky not to have such worries."

In his own personal life, Hargadon was perpetually behind schedule. His children were grown and on their own, and his cluttered bachelor's house cried out for a housekeeper, if only to straighten up the books on the nightstand. "I've got to do that one of these days," he frequently said, never specifying a day. He'd done his Christmas shopping, but not until the very last minute. (Christmas cards had been sent with equal alacrity.) He once got theater tickets weeks in advance, but two hours before the curtain went up, he decided that the work he had to do was more pressing.

At other moments that winter, the stress and the strain of digesting more than twelve thousand applications was relieved, if only for a little while, both intentionally and unintentionally. One day I caught Hargadon with his feet up on the desk. "It just came in," he said excitedly, waving some sort of magazine in the air. It was a mail-order catalog featuring the characters in the comic strip *Doonesbury.*

Another day Hargadon's secretary picked up the phone and was told by the frantic caller that he simply had to speak to the dean. Trained as she was, the secretary said she would first have to know what the subject was. "Tell him I have just one word to say to him," the caller said. When she asked for his name, he refused to give it, repeating that he had but one word to say to Hargadon.

Sighing, the secretary put the caller on hold and pondered whether to put him through—something she seldom did in any case. At the end of the school year, her phone log would show that of the more than two thousand people who tried to call Hargadon that school year, only a tiny fraction had actually spoken to him. The secretary walked into the boss's office and explained to him the bizarre call. Wincing, Hargadon reluctantly picked up the phone.

"Is this Dean Hargadon?" the caller demanded to know. "Yes."

"I have just one word to say to you."

"Yes?"

"Thanks."

The dean was taken aback. The caller explained that he was an alumnus who just wanted to thank Hargadon for admitting a student for whom he had written a letter of recommendation. "All that just to say thank you," the bemused dean said later.

One day in the dead of winter, Hargadon led an unusual staff training session. He began by selecting at random the folder of an applicant who had not yet been evaluated. He opened it and gave his small audience the particulars about a young man: first in his class, star athlete, member of the school band.

The dean's tone suggested that while such credentials are good, they aren't exceptional. But then while this applicant was doing all that, he discovered, he was also working forty hours a week on his family's farm, and sixty during the summer. Suddenly, this was an altogether different kind of candidate—a youth who obviously had a strong work ethic, tremendous self-discipline, and an enormous amount of energy. Being a farm boy also gave him the advantage of coming from a nontraditional background, which would add diversity to a class. After the session was over, the dean shook his head. "Can you believe it was just a folder I pulled out of the pile?" he said.

While the winter had its lighter moments, however, Hargadon always had plenty to be concerned about. He blew a gasket when an alumnus disappeared into the Princeton Club of New York restaurant when he was supposed to be conducting an interview. Not long after, another parent called the admissions office to report that his child also had been scheduled for an alumni interview at the Princeton Club, but the interviewer didn't show up. The very next day, another parent called to say that the same thing had happened to her child in another part of the country.

His temperature rose even higher in response to a letter to the editor in Princeton's alumni magazine. Written by a member of the Class of 1941, it was sarcastic, racist, and sexist in tone: "I was also shocked to learn that only twenty-four percent of the freshman (excuse me—'freshperson') class consists of minority students. If admissions could boost that percentage to ninety percent, then all courses in history, literature, art, music, and foreign languages could be dropped in favor of ethnic studies. Think of the savings in faculty salaries!" These incidents caused Hargadon to blow up, but another problem that winter caused him to brood. The problem was what he called the "fragility" of applicants. He spent a lot of time thinking about it. He talked to faculty members about it. He read applications looking for subtle signs of it. By "fragility," he meant the possibility that an applicant might fall apart under the pressure of competing in the academically rarefied climate of Princeton. He didn't like it when a student he had admitted was brought before the disciplinary committee for drugs, cheating, or whatever. Because the dean sat on the disciplinary committee, he had a front-row seat to his own mistakes.

For example, one applicant wrote that he had taken the greatest satisfaction in achieving his goal of being first in his high school class. Was this, Hargadon wondered, the sort of young person who could hang in against the competition he would encounter at Princeton? How would the young man react if he suddenly were to find himself among the ninety percent of Princeton freshmen who for the first time in their lives find themselves no longer in the top ten percent of their class?

Margaret Greer, associate professor of Romance languages and literatures at Princeton, said that this kind of thinking had had an immediate impact on the kind of students who were admitted. In her capacity as a freshman adviser, Greer saw a dramatic change in students' reactions to lower grades. The year before Hargadon's arrival, students who got B's had reacted by telling her they were going to try to do better. The following year, B's didn't much bother her frosh advisees. "They were just concerned about what courses to take next term. They were excited by the subject matter. They were not judging themselves by the grade that was applied to them." She noticed right away that it was "easier to keep a lively discussion going, because one person's idea would stimulate another person's idea and so on."

Princeton, Hargadon said, "tries to get students out of thinking that (they need to) know the answers to the next test and to get them into thinking, learning how to think critically about anything that would be set before them, most of which they'd have to think about because the answers aren't obvious." Princeton, he said, "puts a premium on the student who is not afraid of walking out of class not knowing the answer."

Or as Michael Mahoney said at the seminar, Hargadon's job is to "spot the students who will ask the best questions, not those who can give the right answers."

☐   ☐   ☐   ❚   ☐

Beyond bright students, Hargadon also looks for the deeper strength of an individual. Today, says Hargadon, most young people haven't undergone a true test of character by the time they are seventeen or eighteen. Therefore, an applicant's integrity and maturity usually must be judged by reading letters of recommendation, studying the student's record of community service, and looking at a seemingly innocuous part of the application: the list of summer and part-time jobs the student has held.

If elite universities were just after a bunch of bright individuals, questions of character wouldn't be so important. But as Duke's Christoph Guttentag puts it, "We're selecting individuals and creating a class simultaneously."

Hargadon sees a student's character as the foundation for leadership. "Leadership doesn't just mean being an officer of an organization," he says. "It means the ability to make decisions that wouldn't have to be made if they pleased everybody. It's the public-spirited—that is, disinterested—person that you hope is going to come out of some of our institutions."

Hargadon bemoans the loss of the character-instilling jobs he says kids used to have. "We went to the drugstore to work behind the counter for four hours an afternoon. We didn't go to look at a whole bunch of magazines that describe what it's like to be our age." To be sure, students' jobs today can be just as arduous. But what Hargadon means by character-building has more to do with what a young person saw while on the job: the grocer who gave credit to the family whose breadwinner was out of work; the butcher who made sure the elderly lady who couldn't get out of the house had her meat delivered.

For some applicants, life itself is arduous enough to be a test of character. Those who have persevered—who have managed not just to stay in school but to do well—often will be admitted ahead of candidates who have done even better but in surroundings much more conducive to learning.

Take the young man whose folder Hargadon started reading one afternoon in December. The boy lived in an inner city, not with his parents but with another relative. Where the boy's parents were the young man didn't know; Mom and Dad had drug problems, and they wandered in and out of his life. The boy's relative had very little money, and at times the boy found himself on the street. And yet unlike many young people in such circumstances, this boy did not drop out of school. On the contrary, school became his refuge, thanks largely to his high school guidance counselor, who wrote in heart-wrenching detail about the boy's difficult childhood. While the young man was qualified for Princeton, his record wasn't exceptional by Princeton's standards. But it was an exceptional record under the circumstances, so much so that before Hargadon had even finished reading the boy's folder, he had admitted the young man in his mind and was thinking about which alumnus he could ask to set up a clothing fund for the boy.

Or take the young man whom Bruce Poch, dean of admissions at Pomona College, came across one year. The young man lived alone under a bridge. When his teachers discovered the boy's situation, they helped him straighten out his life and, in the process, make him an excellent, character-tested candidate for a highly selective institution like Pomona.

The majority of applicants, however, haven't had anything approaching such compelling experiences. For them, Hargadon has a suggestion: Take a year off between high school and college—a gap year, he calls it. A gap year builds character and exposes a young person to a different way of life, he said in a speech to parents of students at Princeton High School.

"There are all kinds of programs that one can participate

in" during the gap year, Hargadon told the parents. "One can go to the American Field Service and spend a year in another country. One can go off and help build a cabin in the mountains. One can work on a sheep ranch in Australia. All sorts of things. One can go to a foreign country and concentrate on the language of that country, working in a menial way to earn the money to live there." It's been his own experience, the dean said, that young people who take a year off between high school and college enter college with more perspective and maturity, and "slightly more" wisdom. "If I had my way," he added, "I think it would be great" to admit a class of students who, almost without exception, had had a gap year.

In fact Hargadon himself benefited from not just one, but several gap years. The last paragraph of his official biography reads: "Having begun his freshman year at Haverford College at age 21, he [Hargadon] is comfortable with the notion that he probably would not have admitted himself, at age 17, to either Haverford, Swarthmore, Stanford, or Princeton." To be sure, it isn't necessary to wait until after high school to have a character-building, perspective-enhancing gap year. "Here's a student who was in the American Field Service in Brazil," Hargadon said one day while reviewing applications. "Great to see students [like that]. It isn't that she comes back a Portuguese expert. It isn't that she comes back a Brazilian expert. It's that that kind of experience in another country puts perspective on where she is now." Indeed, in her application the young woman talked about women's inequality in Brazil.

This applicant probably would be admitted, Hargadon said.

While it's hard to find eighteen-year-old applicants who have undergone tests of character, once in a while it's easy to spot one who has—and who has failed. One day the mother of a student who had been admitted early action to Princeton called to tell Hargadon that her son had also applied to and been accepted by an institution that had a binding early decision program. The mother said she understood that her child had made a mistake, but she begged the dean not to withdraw her child's offer of admission, because Princeton was where her son really wanted to go. Hargadon listened, but he didn't sympathize with the mother. When these things happen, he later said, and it looks to him as if the family is unsophisticated about the differences between early action and early decision, he will make a call to the admissions head of the other institution to see whether the candidate might be released from his or her obligation. This time, no call was made.

CHAPTER □ **17**

"**D**o you know who these kids are really competing against?" Hargadon asked me, pointing at a stack of application folders.

"They're competing against the kids who are here.

"How about a student who founded the first high school chapter of Habitat for Humanity and was the first high school member of the international board? That's who they're competing against. They're competing against a highly recruited tight end. They're competing against a cellist who already is a world-concert person with a CD. They're competing against a young migrant worker's daughter from California.

"How many [colleges] have the young woman—young black woman, as it turns out—who set the record for selling Girl Scout cookies . . . and then had businesses inviting her to talk about sales and wrote a book about it before she got to Princeton? You don't see too many." What if she had only set the record? I asked. "The thing is," he said, laughing, "it was a humongous record."

A couple of his examples sounded familiar to me. I fished out of my files the form letter Hargadon had sent to alumni interviewers the previous year, the one in which he had thanked us for our efforts. The letter said: "Among literally hundreds and hundreds of noteworthy accomplishments of [the next freshman] class, space allows mention of just a few to give you the flavor of the class: the first-prize winner of the Westinghouse Science Competition, the winner of the International Physics Olympiad held in Warsaw, Poland, an Olympic class swimmer (and daughter of a P '60), the published author of a children's book, the founder of the first high school chapter of Habitat for Humanity and first high school student to serve on the International Board of Advisors to that organization, the National Youth President of the National Association of Negro Musicians who is also a National Endowment for the Humanities Scholarship winner, a young woman from Surrey, England, who came to Princeton from the Royal Ballet School to which she was selected after completing high school two years ago, a young black man from Bophutatsawana, South Africa, who spent last year at the Gilman School in Baltimore, and [a] young woman from a small town in Oregon who in addition to graduating first in her class and being Editor-in-Chief of the yearbook, rebuilds cars and drives in demolition derby events! That's just for starters."

Starters?!

Says the dean: "Most [colleges] would give their right arm to have the kid we can't admit. I'm really spoiled."

For the current crop of parents and applicants, it's a fairly intimidating list. At the same time, however, there is something reassuring about this roll call. Given the group's extraordinary range of achievement, it is fair to say that, first and foremost, all of these young people succeeded in getting into

Princeton by being themselves, by following their own muse, working hard at something they loved to do. Only a couple on the list appear to be superstars. Most simply seem to be smart, talented kids who were motivated to do something special with their talents.

In his letter to prospective applicants, Hargadon strongly advises students to "just be yourself" on the application. Unable to resist exercising his wry sense of humor, the dean adds, "I confess that every time I offer that advice, I remember the comment that Mark Twain made: 'Telling a person to be himself is the worst advice you can give to some people.' Still, that's my advice."

"Many candidates are driven to make themselves look like they know as much and have accomplished as much as possible," Hargadon said one day after wading through yet another pile of applications. "I think it's the rare student in our schools who isn't worried about impressing and who has a very good perspective on life and is comfortable admitting what it is they don't know."

In the introduction to a book about college essay writing, Hargadon wrote, "In my most plaintive moments as an admissions dean, I could be heard stalking the office corridors shouting, 'Where the hell are the Huckleberry Finns?' " Such an explosion, he wrote, usually occurred after he had read a lot of applications "that left me convinced we had cornered the market on saints and scholars, none of whom had ever stumbled, faltered, or failed at anything, and few of whom seemed real." While applicants are advised to put their best foot forward, he added, "I must confess that I always liked the ones who put *both* feet forward."

Just how much Hargadon likes a two-footed candidate

came out at the meeting for alumni interviewers back in September. After showing the graphic that illustrated how many valedictorians get rejected, the dean described a candidate whom he had admitted the previous year because he found the young man to be particularly "compelling." What had made this applicant compelling was an essay he had written, which Hargadon paraphrased as follows: "I am the worst soccer player on the worst soccer team in the state. I have been on the team four years, and I've gotten into four games." Smiling from ear to ear, the dean told his audience, "That guy is either the greatest, most refreshing candidate I've ever seen, or he really knows just how to get to me."

Selecting a candidate because he's a rotten soccer player may sound ridiculous. But in the act of admitting what it is he doesn't know how to do, the young man has suggested that he will be open to the "active" learning that goes on in a first-rate university. Whatever else he may be, this young man is clearly not an empty slate. He is open-minded without being empty-headed. (Of course, he also had the necessary grades and scores.)

There is another way in which Huck Finn epitomizes what elite universities like Princeton are looking for in a candidate. Not only is it by far the most subjective of all the subjective qualities that an elite institution finds desirable, it also is one of the most important.

This is the matter of whether the university considers a candidate a good "match." What this means is whether the candidate is truly interested in learning for learning's sake. "Do you want to come to college and get a 4.0 and graduate Phi Beta Kappa, or do you want to learn as much about astrophysics as you can?" is how Hargadon put it one time, adding, "We would love to see as many students as possible who are interested in learning for the sake of learning."

While such students reflect Hargadon's own personality, they also reflect the essential purpose of many of America's top universities. As liberal arts institutions, these universities are concerned with educating the "whole" person, not with training him or her for a specific profession or career. As Woodrow Wilson put it when he was president of Princeton a century ago, "We must deal in college with the spirits of men, not with their fortunes."

Hargadon sees a young person's college years as a raft ride down a long and hopefully twisting river that's full of surprises in terms of new knowledge and personal growth. As long as students are in the middle of the river, they are free to explore, to learn for the sake of learning. Hargadon wants to keep young people from coming ashore any sooner than they have to. Which is not to suggest that he views mankind as stupid or venal. Rather, the shore is for him the equivalent of the job market, of one's ultimate and inescapable need to make a living.

"We try to distinguish between who wants to come here for the learning," he told me, "and who wants to come here to get another set of top credentials on top of the ones they have in order to do the next step."

Hargadon has another watery metaphor for college education, taken, he said, from a sign outside a bookstore in New York City: "College is a place where wise men and women fish."

At Princeton, the wise-fish-here view permeates the thinking even of the university's director of career services, who believes that college should be a time for exploration and self-discovery, not a time for carving out careers. At a February seminar for parents of Princeton students on the "relationship between academic work and careers," Minerva Reed said Princeton students are advised to "follow your heart's desire. A career will follow," though not necessarily with the first job after graduation. Reed said that while her office brings in some three hundred organizations a year to recruit Princeton students for jobs, she sees her job as being to help students make "life choices."

Reed's comments drew heated responses from the audience. Indeed, a number of parents in the oak-paneled lecture hall voiced concern over the seemingly strong element of "happenstance" in career planning at Princeton. A father said it sounded as if Princeton believes that "careers don't happen while you're planning them." Bewildered, the father added, "Maybe I'm the one who needs counseling."

That the best, most personally satisfying careers "happen" when one follows one's heart's desire was the university's message that day, and it was delivered to the parents by three middle-aged Princeton graduates who had been invited to speak.

The first speaker, a 1970 graduate, told the parents that when he arrived at Princeton, he discovered "a huge variety of things that interested me." While he had arrived planning to be an English major, he had "shopped around" and "fell in love" with geology. He became a geology major and, after graduation, went to work for a museum, which sent him on an archaeological expedition to Afghanistan. While on that dig, he had a lot of free time, during which he took pictures of the people and the countryside. Photography was something he had never done before, but his experience in Afghanistan got him so interested that he took a succession of newspaper jobs. In 1974 he started his own photography business, which he still runs today.

The second speaker, a 1971 graduate, said he arrived at Princeton thinking he wanted to be an engineer but almost immediately switched to something he found more interesting—physics. He decided he wanted to teach physics, so he enrolled in the university's teacher preparation placement program. Then, however, he took a course in computer programming, which led to a summer job, which led to a full-time job after graduation. The job involved doing computerized educational research for a nationally known firm. "I didn't know I was into a career until ten years later," he said.

The third speaker, a 1972 graduate, said he had come to Princeton thinking he was going to become a doctor. But in trying to find a major that "matched my curiosity," he found anthropology. Since no anthropology major was offered at the time, he became an "independent concentrator," carving out his own course of study. The more anthropology taught him about human behavior, the more he realized that social counseling appealed to him. While still an undergraduate, he worked with local black children on "ways to express themselves that were not destructive or self-destructive." After graduation, he taught at an inner-city school, then went back to get a master's degree in education. He was currently involved in what he called "social action" in the inner city. One of his projects provides transportation for relatives of prison inmates so that they can visit their loved ones. "If you can understand anthropology," he told the Princeton parents, "it will help you with whatever you want to do."

When the speakers were finished, however, the parents were still concerned. Just before the meeting broke up, one father said exasperatedly that that morning he had tried, and failed, to get his daughter to tell him, "What are you going to do with it?"—the "it" being her foreign language major.

For parents who want their kids to go to a college like Princeton, too much emphasis on "planning" (the "right" college and the "right" major, followed by the "right" graduate school followed by the "right" career) would appear to be counterproductive because it may prevent their kids from doing what Hargadon and Princeton want them to do most: be themselves; follow their own muse; get out on their own and develop maturity, perspective, a slightly different way of seeing the world.

One student who did just this was the young woman from Oregon who had graduated first in her class and been the editor of her yearbook. The eldest of four girls, her father owned an auto-repair business and wouldn't let her drive a car until she had learned how to restore one. She, her father, and her mother all had driven in demolition derby events held during the summer near her home. She also had competed in drag races. When Princeton accepted her, she became the first person in her town to attend an Ivy League school.

Upon her arrival at Princeton, the promise this young woman had shown as an applicant was richly borne out. She became her dormitory's representative on her college council. She made regular calls on the elderly at a local rest home. She became distribution manager of a bimonthly student publication. She joined a committee charged with improving the quality of food served on campus. In short, the young woman was doing everything the dean of admissions of an elite university hopes a student will do. She was "fishing" in the "bookstore" that is a liberal arts university. She was providing the glue that holds a community together. She was showing a leader's concern for people other than herself.

CHAPTER ▯ **18**

Even though most high school seniors in the United States would have been happy to trade places with them, by mid-February each of my four remaining kids was completely miserable.

Not long after Nora played Beat the Clock with her applications, she received a letter from a small private college. At first she thought it would be just another of the dozens of letters she had received urging her to apply. But when she read it, she discovered that this school was so impressed by her academic record that it was offering her a full scholarship—a free four-year ride.

Pretty much the same thing happened to Mark. A music professor from a Midwestern college had heard him play at the camp he attended over the summer and was impressed by his talent. One night Mark got a telephone call from one of the school's administrators, who wanted to know what it would take to get Mark to apply. Before Mark could answer, the administrator asked if he would like to fly in for a weekend visit, all expenses paid by the college.

Meanwhile, both Sirrka and Lucy were offered scholarships by their respective state universities. But none of the kids had any interest in attending the colleges that were so eager to accept them. Nora simply crumpled up her letter and tossed it into a wastebasket. Mark, seeming to represent the group, explained that he passed up the free plane ride because the Midwestern school just didn't have the "shiny prestige" he wanted. "Perhaps," he said, "I could be just as well off and just as happy at a college without a big name. But I've bought into the idea that a big name school will give me security."

Whether or not a big name school still buys the security it once did, the kids were right not to want to settle at this point for a "safety" school. Still, all of them were blind to the underlying significance of these scholarship offers. The offers were evidence that, regardless of whether they got into their first-choice schools, they were still fine students with very bright futures. There was other evidence for this that the kids didn't see. A number of teachers, for instance, vied for the honor of writing Lucy's teacher reports.

By buying in to the idea of "prestige" over the best match, the students set themselves up for a winter of discontent that would quite possibly be followed by an unforgettable final rejection by their first-choice school. At that point they would have to settle for a slightly less prominent college—one, to be sure, that most kids can only dream of attending. If Sirrka, for instance, didn't get into Princeton, in all likelihood she would have to "settle" for either the University of Pennsylvania or Johns Hopkins.

Despite her enviable fallback position, however, the thought of not going to Princeton was unimaginable to Sirrka. Even after the early decision rejection reduced her to tears in her high school library, she remained emotionally hooked. She was on the campus nearly every day, and while familiarity often breeds contempt, in Sirrka's case it led to enchantment. After her language class let out, she often strolled around the grounds, dreamily listening to the cacophony of music blaring out of dormitory windows, imagining herself part of next year's freshman class. Sirrka was convinced that Princeton was the only place she could be happy.

But with her first-semester grades, her odds of getting in were not looking good: A's in English, French, and computer programming, a B in biology, and a B minus in calculus. She would be lucky to be in the top ten percent of her class.

Still, Sirrka was proud of her grades. It had been a tough transition to the new school in her senior year, and she felt she had done well. Her counselor agreed that she had worked hard. "It's not a bad report card," he told me. "But it's not the one she needed."

Sirrka wasn't the only one who went out of her way to make herself miserable. Lucy went to her physics teacher, who also was head of her school's science department, to ask him about the summer school for gifted science students. After describing what had happened to her there, Lucy asked him, in so many words, How can I be doing so well in this high school, yet be so far behind those other kids?

The teacher didn't beat around the bush. The plain fact was, he said, that a lot of teachers in her high school weren't that great and that the students paid the price. Lucy had already known this but had thought that forcing the truth out of someone else would make her feel better. It didn't. All she felt afterward was an overwhelming sense of regret. If only I could start all over at a private school, she said to herself.

Lucy was also feeling yet another strain. Her boyfriend, a graduate of the same high school that she attended, was already in college and wanted her to go somewhere close by to him. No college Lucy had applied to filled the bill. As a result, going out on a date with him only added to the pressure she felt.

Having been banished by Lucy's mother in December in order to let Lucy concentrate on filling out her college applications, her boyfriend was never far away during January and February. On Friday nights now, Bobby took her out to dinner and a movie. Lucy tried to keep the conversation moving, talking about friends, school, *anything* besides their relationship and where it was heading.

But Bobby kept bringing up the subject of marriage until, finally, Lucy found herself blurting out, "I'm too young!"

Afterward, Lucy felt enormously relieved. She realized that leaving her relationship with Bobby as unsettled as her college plans had been making senior year doubly difficult. She couldn't do anything about the latter, but at least now she'd laid to rest the former.

▯ ▯ ▯ ▮ ▯

Nora did not have such complications. Her idea of a big Saturday night was to load up at the video store and settle in with a big bowl of ice cream. But even when she was just sitting and relaxing, Nora could not keep her mind off college.

Nora was haunted by an episode from the end of her junior year. Just as Lucy had gone to a summer school for gifted students, Nora had been in the running for a similar program, but the honor had gone to another student who had lower grades but who, in Nora's opinion at least, was "connected." (Even Nora's counselor was puzzled as to why Nora hadn't been selected.) Nora's recurring nightmare was that she would be passed over by Princeton in favor of someone with lower grades but was "connected," probably a son or daughter of an alumnus or alumna. The fact that the son of a Princeton alumnus in her high school class had been admitted in the fall only made the nightmare worse.

Neither did it help that almost every minute of every day at school, somebody around Nora was saying dejectedly, "I just know I won't get in" to Harvard, or Princeton, or Yale. While eating lunch in the cafeteria with her friends, Nora would talk herself into a depression so deep that not even a gallon of ice cream would have cheered her up.

One day in March, she and I sat down with her guidance counselor in his office. "The whole thing is just so unfair!" she almost screamed, dynamiting the self-control she was trying to project, even as others around her were losing their heads. "These colleges have absolute control over my life, and there's nothing I can do about it. I'd like to think it's really all just a matter of luck. But if Princeton rejects me, I may feel really awful." Then she moaned, "Oh, God, I don't want to go through something like this ever again."

▢ ▢ ▢ ▮ ▢

I wanted to look beyond the superstars that Dean Hargadon had been telling me about and meet some of the more "normal" undergraduates at Princeton. John V. Fleming, a professor of English and longtime master of Wilson College, was happy to oblige.

Snow covered the campus the day we lunched together in the Wilson College dining hall, with five students—three freshmen, a junior, and a senior. (The latter two served as resident advisers.) There were three women and two men. The women came from Long Island, a Washington–Baltimore suburb, and Texas. The men came from New England and California. The woman from Texas was Hispanic and a minority recruiter for the admissions office.

"A lot of my friends who applied to Princeton and didn't get in, didn't have any kind of talent," said the woman from Long Island, Sharon. "I did. My talent was writing. I sent in a writing portfolio." Not coincidentally, she had won a prestigious national writing award.

One of the young men also thought he had gotten in on individual talent. "I played in a national symphony orchestra," John said, adding: "All my relatives told me to stick to one thing and be good at it."

At first the woman from Texas, Anita, said, "I got in because I'm Hispanic." But later in the conversation, she said she thought she had gotten in because she was "well-rounded," including being good at sports. "I don't think there was anything special that I did. It was just a combination of things."

The other male student, Dave, said he thought he had gotten in primarily because of his essay, which he described as an offbeat look at someone trying to become a writer. His mother works in the admissions office of another highly selective university and showed her son's college essay to her coworkers. By the time he sent in his Princeton application, he said, "I already knew that the essay was good enough to get me in" to the selective college where his mother worked.

The last young woman's parents hadn't been around when she was a senior in high school, having obligations that required them to be abroad. Janice went to a selective private school that, as she put it, cost her parents "major bucks." She, too, viewed herself as well-rounded. The reason she singled out to account for her being admitted was the high-quality counseling she had received at her private school. "My guidance counselor was really, really good. She knew what she was doing and she was always there to help. She wasn't even a guidance counselor; she was a 'college counselor.' "

When I asked the others, all of whom had attended public high schools, if they had been beneficiaries of good counseling, they looked at me as if I were crazy. Anita said, "I think counselors in my part of the country try to discourage kids [from applying to Ivy League schools] because they don't know about them. I had to learn about Princeton on my own." The only mildly favorable comment came from John, who said: "My counselor tried to help me, but with hundreds of other students she was responsible for, she didn't have enough time."

I asked the entire group, "How important do you think your grades and test scores were?"

Said John: "If you have a really high grade-point average and low test scores, it means you work hard but you're not that bright. If you have really high test scores but a low GPA, it means you're really bright but you're lazy. You need correlating scores in order to look natural."

Said another: "I know kids who had great test scores who didn't get in. They didn't focus enough on their applications. They relied too much on SAT review courses."

Since the purpose of an alumni interview is also to explain about a school and encourage students, if accepted, to enroll, I then asked, "What effect did the alumni interview have on your decision to come?"

They laughed. Sharon said she didn't even have her interview until three months after she was admitted. Two said they had seriously thought about not coming because of the lousy impression their interviewer had made. "He didn't ask me any questions. He just wanted to talk about himself," said Dave. "He was so out of touch, he hadn't even heard of one of the other colleges I was applying to," said one of the women. (The college in question was Northwestern University, hardly a state secret.)

Then I asked: "Do you think luck played a role in your being here?"

Said Sharon: "When I was eight years old, my father told me that he wanted me to go to Princeton." He wasn't an alum; he just wanted to be the father of one. Because of that paternal pressure, "at first I didn't want to go here at all," but preferred a city school. Only after she had decided to go to Princeton did her mother confess to deliberately not having mailed in the other application. (Amazingly, mother and daughter were still on speaking terms.)

The discussion also revealed just how personally destructive the college admissions process can be. Janice and her best friend, she said, had shared a dream to attend Princeton together. When Janice got in and her friend did not, the friend never spoke to her again. Shortly after Dave was accepted by Princeton, his book bag mysteriously disappeared. A year later, he found out from a friend that his former best friend, who had stopped talking to him after being rejected by Princeton, had secretly stolen the book bag and thrown it off a bridge and into a river.

While these incidents were completely understandable to the group, they baffled me, given that the two "losers" had gotten into highly respected, highly selective colleges that didn't happen to be named Princeton, Harvard, or Yale. What I didn't understand, the group told me, was that for most kids who have been told by parents, teachers, and friends that they are *the* best, there are only three colleges in the world. (The Californian added Stanford.) The group nodded in agreement when Janice said, "All my teachers and friends and relatives always said, 'You'll have no trouble getting into Princeton.' I was really scared. I think I would rather have heard, 'Well, if you don't get in, there are other options.' "

□   □   □   ▮   □

The wide variety of talents in this small sampling illustrates the point Hargadon had made about what it takes to people the residential community that is Princeton University.

Hargadon says he is often amazed at everything that's needed to, as he puts it, "man this operation." Given Princeton's relatively small size, he says, "I think we expect more out of a higher proportion of our incoming freshman class than many colleges do. Meaning that some are going to have a background in journalism and work for the *Princetonian*.

Some are going to have a background in community service activities and lead the Student Volunteer Council. And, you know, there are more than thirty varsity sports."

In a speech to Princeton High School parents, Hargadon explained how the need to man the operation meshes with Princeton's educational philosophy. "We're applying an overview in terms of the objectives of the university," he said. These objectives are both academic and nonacademic. Students who are admitted primarily because they fulfill the university's academic objectives have "the potential to be real scholars. Not just [to get] high grades or high test scores or [to be] first in the class. But four years from now [to be] one of the top scholars in the physics department or the math department." Of students admitted primarily because they satisfy a nonacademic objective, Hargadon will think that he or she "may not be the top student in the class, but [he or she] is going to be the top quarterback in the class, or the top cellist in the class, and so forth." Some candidates are themselves a package. "We also keep an eye on, 'Here's a great student and also an outstanding cellist.' We're aware that when that spring concert comes around, [we're] going to need some instruments."

I subsequently asked Hargadon how many academic and nonacademic objectives Princeton has. "I've never counted them up," he replied. "But think about all the different minority groups that are interested in their being fairly represented. Think of international students. Think of trying to attract really able students from a different variety of socioeconomic backgrounds. And you're lucky every once in a while [because you find] a candidate [with] quite a different background

[who] will make a contribution to the class by being from a coal-mining family, and, to boot, they're also an excellent cellist."

Asked whether Princeton has too many objectives, Hargadon said, "At times it seems that way." Then: "There certainly are times in the process when you feel that you do not have as many places in the class as you have objectives. And by objectives I mean everything from a given department really wanting specific kinds of candidates . . . to the orchestra wanting enough players, to everybody wanting students who are going to participate in drama and theater and dance. . . . We try to get so much done in such a small class. We have to wend our way through the narrowest of gates."

While most selective colleges have these multiple objectives, there are exceptions, including Reed College in Oregon. Reed admissions head Bob Mansueto doesn't have intercollegiate sports to worry about. Neither, he says, does he feel compelled to populate academic departments and student musical groups. "The music department lives with what comes in." Reed, Mansueto adds, wants students for whom the library will be the center of their college experience.

No matter what a candidate has to offer, it helps to have Lady Luck at the helm to get through selective colleges' gates. First, it helps to have the obvious luck of being born on the right street, which nearly always determines the schools one gets to attend, which in turn determines the quality of one's academic preparation and the support one receives when applying to college from teachers and guidance counselors.

It also helps to have luck in who else is applying to the same university the same year. Over and above the luck involved in the number of applicants accepted for whom that university isn't their first choice, there is the luck involved in whether the university community is in need of the applicant's particular skills and talents that year. One year an institution may need virtuoso violinists for its orchestra. The next year it may have two or three virtuoso violinists in its freshman class. If an applicant's skill, his project, is playing the violin, it's great to be applying that first year but not so great the second.

To be sure, the university community has many needs every year; it needs enough students for each of its academic departments and enough athletes for each of its sports teams. But here again, luck plays a role. One year a candidate may be the best-looking future physics major or quarterback in the applicant pool. The next year several others may look better. In his speech to the Princeton Club of Philadelphia, Hargadon rhetorically asked, "How can you let people know before the process starts that there's an element of luck in this? The part you can't control is how many other people like yourselves decided to apply to Princeton this year."

CHAPTER □ 19

E very parent whose child gets rejected by a highly selective university is convinced that a mistake was made. One father who years later still thinks his daughter should have been admitted to Princeton is none other than Princeton president Harold Shapiro, whose daughter applied and was rejected when he was an economics professor at Michigan. "My daughter was, in my judgment, in every way qualified. She would have made an excellent student."

But while Shapiro the parent says Princeton made a mistake, Shapiro the university president insists that Princeton's admissions process is fair. But what *fair* means to an elite university is different from what it means to a parent. Because parents are concerned only about their own children, to parents *fairness* means admitting the most qualified individuals; the definition of *qualified* will vary from one parent to the next. But universities are concerned with putting together a community of people, as well as addressing social and their own institutional needs, so to a university *fairness* means striking a balance among the institution's multiple objectives. As a result, a process that an elite university is convinced is fair, many parents, teachers, and guidance counselors will be equally convinced is unfair.

One day Hargadon was reviewing the folder of a young man who was an officer of the student government in his high school, an outstanding athlete, and the winner of a prestigious national science award. The young man was also the child of a Princeton graduate, thereby making him a "legacy" applicant. The young man was one of those applicants on whose folders Hargadon wrote, "Marked for Admit," meaning that when it was time for the final committee meeting, the young man's admission would be a formality. The dean said he was thinking of adding a P.S. at the bottom of this young man's letter of acceptance, something along the lines of: "The fact that your father went here didn't make a damned difference."

The fact remains, however, that being a legacy generally does make a difference in a young person's chances of getting into a highly selective American university. Princeton is typical of elite institutions in that its acceptance rate for legacies is more than double the acceptance rate for the applicant group as a whole. For the Princeton Class of 1997, there were 396 legacy candidates, of whom 172 were admitted, a forty-three percent acceptance rate, compared with just a fifteen percent or so acceptance rate for the applicant group as a whole. (Take out the legacy group, and of course the overall acceptance rate was even lower.)

Being a legacy candidate is always an advantage, but the only way for a legacy candidate to know just how much of an edge he or she has when applying to Mom's or Dad's alma mater is to examine not just the school's written but, more important, its unwritten policy regarding legacy candidates.

In general, elite schools' written policies state only that preference will be shown, but that unqualified candidates will not be admitted just because their folks are graduates. Unwritten policies must be pieced together based on historical data and other information that must be asked for specifically.

For example, by piecing together the information that Harvard and Princeton admit better than forty percent of all legacy candidates but fewer than fifteen percent of total applicants, one discovers that, statistically speaking, a candidate has roughly a three times better chance of being admitted to those schools if his or her father or mother went there. At Pennsylvania, about fifty-five percent of legacy candidates are admitted, compared with about thirty-two percent of total applicants. Thus, a Penn legacy appears to be less of an advantage than a Harvard or Princeton legacy. Actually, however, a Penn legacy has an even better statistical chance of being admitted than a Harvard or Princeton legacy—*if* he or she applies at the right time. Penn tells its legacies to apply during its early decision period in order to demonstrate a real desire to come to Penn. (If admitted early to Penn, a candidate must attend.) Roughly sixty-five percent to seventy percent of Penn legacy candidates who apply early are accepted, an advantage that falls way off if a legacy candidate waits to apply during the regular admissions period—even if that spring legacy applicant is gung-ho about attending Penn.

Legacy candidates who apply to Pomona College also have a better chance of being admitted than they might think. That's because Pomona's admissions head, Bruce Poch, tries to, as he puts it, "scare" the lesser qualified into *not* applying by publishing a class profile in the alumni magazine.

In general, legacies to all highly selective colleges and universities enjoy a significant hidden advantage in admissions because, as Rice's Barry McFarland notes, as a group, they are better educated than the overall applicant pool, thanks to the educational values their usually successful parents have passed on to them.

Still, just as legacies at some elite schools enjoy a greater advantage than it seems at first, at other schools they have less of an advantage than it would appear. Rice's acceptance rate for legacies is only ten percent higher than for the applicant group as a whole. But Rice legacies can be forgiven for thinking their chances are better than that. When any applicant is put on a school's wait list, it's only natural for him or her to think there's still a bona-fide chance to get in. But, as previously mentioned, Rice puts some legacies on its wait list for "political" reasons.

The pressure on private colleges and universities to admit a significant percentage of alumni children is great and growing. As he lunched in the posh dining room for faculty and administrators, Princeton's vice president for public affairs, Robert Durkee, explained the predicament that even well-endowed private institutions such as Princeton feel they are in today.

"Just look at the numbers. Look at the fact that eighty percent of college students in the country are not going to private colleges and universities. And some growing percentage of people in the Congress did not go to private colleges and universities. You've got to believe that the amount of public support for private colleges and universities is not going to increase and probably will decrease over a period of time. Well, one of the things that means is that the pressure on these institutions to cultivate support from private individuals is going to increase. One way you do that is to retain family ties to the institution. And one way you do that is to continue to enroll some significant fraction of alumni children."

At Princeton as at many other elite schools, alumni contributions are already indispensable. During the 1992–93 school year, the university's Annual Giving campaign raised more than $19 million from alumni, parents, and friends of the university. This represented roughly ten percent of the university's overall budget for educational and general expenses.

Like Durkee, Hargadon feels legacy preference is needed for "building the loyalty to the institution." Says the dean: "In return for those resources, some preference will be exercised on an all-things-being-equal basis at the admissions level. Not necessarily for the one who gave the building, but in general."

At some elite institutions, an applicant whose family is in a position to give a building is singled out for special handling, even if the applicant isn't a legacy. Duke's admissions office "takes into account" what the development office (aka the fundraising office) says, according to admissions director Christoph Guttentag. A "small number" of "sensitive" cases, Guttentag says, are referred by the admissions office to a committee of senior administrators.

Hargadon jokes that he probably costs Princeton several millions each year by not admitting kids on the list sent over by Princeton's development office. Indirectly, he conceded that being a legacy gives an applicant an advantage that other applicants don't have when he mentioned writing the P.S. to a legacy, "The fact that your father went here didn't make a damned difference."

Also indirectly, Hargadon concedes that admitting a high percentage of legacy applicants works against the school's other admissions objectives. Legacy preference is "one additional criterion" by which candidates are judged, the dean says; "if you are exercising that criterion as one additional criterion in their cases, you don't get to say, 'Boy, here's a great kid [from a high] school [from which] we haven't admitted anyone in twenty years.'" Without legacy preference, he adds, "you would have more freedom for other choices."

Nowhere in the admissions process are what the public considers fair and what an elite university considers fair more at odds than in the preference shown to legacies. From the public point of view, there simply is no way to justify admitting a legacy even in part because he is a legacy, instead of a great kid from a high school that hasn't gotten anyone into Princeton in twenty years.

From a societal point of view, legacy preference seems wrong for a number of reasons. First, because it is a "hereditary" privilege, legacy preference is antithetical to the democratic thinking upon which the United States was founded. Second, because many graduates of elite universities make a lot of money, legacy preference tends to give students from affluent families yet another advantage over students born into less favorable circumstances. Third, because an elite university's alumni are predominantly white, legacy preference is mostly a white man's privilege, perpetuating the pattern of discrimination that existed prior to affirmative action.

These are powerful reasons to support doing what Nathaniel Hawthorne suggested in *The House of the Seven Gables*: "Once in every half-century, at longest, a family should be merged into the great, obscure mass of humanity, and forget all about its ancestors." If the only justification for legacy preference were that it attracted money to an institution, I would favor federal and state governments forcing private colleges and universities to abolish it by threatening to withdraw taxpayer support of these institutions.

However, in and of itself, building loyalty to an institution is a worthy objective; the idea of community shouldn't end when a class graduates. Building loyalty to schools that are perhaps the last best chance for the continuation of the "melting pot" ideal seems an especially worthy objective.

Some elite college alumni would argue that they "earn" a legacy preference for their children by writing a check to their alma mater each year. Others would argue that they earn that privilege by volunteering their time on behalf of fund-raising and other university activities.

Over time, as graduates of highly selective institutions become a more and more diversified group, the pool of legacy applicants should reflect that diversity and act to perpetuate student diversity at the nation's best colleges and universities in the twenty-first century.

The impetus behind diversity, however, is also under attack. As we know all too well from recent political debates, a rapidly growing number of Americans view affirmative action with hostility.

In explaining why they think affirmative action in college admissions is unfair, middle- and upper-middle-class families I talked to tended, not surprisingly, to emphasize that every candidate should stand on his or her own merits. It galled them to hear that some minority applicants got into Princeton with lower grades and test scores than some white candidates. It satisfied them not a whit that the same percentage of minority students as white students admitted by Princeton are in the top ten percent of their respective high school classes.

▯ ▯ ▯ ▮ ▯

One day, Hargadon spent over an hour on the telephone being interviewed for a story about affirmative action in higher education by a reporter for a major news magazine. Toward the end of the interview, Hargadon was startled when the reporter asked him what he meant by the term "Pell grant"—one of the cornerstones of federal policy, a grant of up to $2,300 for financially needy undergraduates.

While the conversation was still fresh in his mind, Hargadon drafted a seven-page, single-spaced, typewritten fact sheet, "Affirmative Action in Undergraduate Admissions." The document's subtext was the difficulty of trying to juggle a democracy's sometimes-conflicting notions of fairness. "We treat each applicant individually. We look for individual strengths, both academic and personal." But "it is also the case that many . . . minority students generally find themselves in the high schools with the fewest resources, and in the least affluent of our communities." Overall, Hargadon defended affirmative action, even as he regretted that it was, in his opinion, still necessary in higher education.

"Well," he wrote, "had you asked me back in 1964 just how long I thought it would be necessary to have affirmative action, I think I might have suggested a decade or so, time enough, I would have imagined, for the results of affirmative action—the increased access to places like Princeton for minority students—to have had positive effects on the aspirations and motivations and preparation of students just then entering elementary school. That we have increased access to college, or at least college choice, for many minority students seems to me undeniable. But it also seems to me that the trickle-down effects have been nowhere near as substantial as we had hoped for. I think the inequalities in schooling are far more severe now than back in the 1960s, and those inequalities continue to disproportionately fall upon students from the very minority backgrounds on which our affirmative actions have been focused. I think it will be quite a while before affirmative action no longer seems necessary."

One out of every four or five students who enrolls at Princeton is an American minority. In the Class of 1995, that broke down as follows: six percent black, seven percent Hispanic, one half of one percent Native American, and eleven percent Asian-American.

"It's as important," Hargadon wrote, "to know what affirmative action at Princeton is not, as to know what it is. It is *not* a matter of admitting unqualified students. It is not a remedial or special admission program. It does *not* involve quotas. We do not set aside a specific number of places in the freshman class for minority students. It does *not* represent a deviation from, or an exception to, some presumed single admission standard or criterion according to which all other admission decisions are made."

On this topic Hargadon has felt the wrath of many and not just the disappointed parents of white applicants who always bombard his office with angry letters for weeks after the letters of acceptance and rejection are mailed out in the spring. One year the dean got a letter from a rejected candidate who was Asian-American. The candidate charged that the rejection was racially motivated. The letter wasn't just angry, it was venomous. Hargadon penned an equally irate denial that likely did nothing to change the applicant's mind.

While there was no way to read that ex-candidate's mind, it is easy to imagine that he had been influenced by the fact that affirmative action at Princeton technically includes only blacks, Hispanics, and Native Americans. If Asian-Americans are considered "minority Americans" when the university totals up the numbers, why aren't they included under affirmative action?

"I believe," wrote Hargadon, "that affirmative action at Princeton came to focus on students from these particular backgrounds partly as the result of history, partly as the result of social forces, and partly because the University determined that increasing access by students from these particular backgrounds to educational opportunities of the sort offered by Princeton would help to address a critical social need, and also would enhance the educational experience of *all* undergraduates. Initially, the University's affirmative action focused on Black students and after four or five years came to include Puerto Rican, Mexican-American, and Native American students. It is students from these particular backgrounds who, for a variety of historical and cultural reasons, most obviously were not applying to or enrolling in institutions like Princeton prior to the affirmative action efforts that got under way in the mid-1960s."

Nora would disagree with Hargadon's explanation.

In mid-December, just days after the elite schools sent out their early action letters, Nora had participated in a group discussion with other students in her high school who had either just gotten into a selective institution or who, like herself, hoped to attend one. Having arranged the discussion with the help of Nora's guidance counselor, Stanley Humphries, I was seated at one end of a long conference table. Facing me at the other end were Nora and an African-American girl named Alice Mayhew, who had just been accepted early by Yale, one of the schools to which Nora planned to apply. At one point, Alice said, "People get mad if they think you're going to get in and they're not. We had to fill out this thing for guidance about what makes you 'different.' I put down that I'm black. People said to me, 'Oh, my God, the admissions person is going to love you.' They got mad at me for being black! Excuse me?"

Nora's body language—her arms folded tightly across her chest, eyes straight down—suggested that she was one of the angry ones. Some time later, I asked Nora whether she thought that Alice's being black had given her an unfair advantage. She said yes. "I'm Asian," she said. "We've been discriminated against, too." Her point: Why should one minority get treated differently from another?

Pennsylvania's admissions dean, Lee Stetson, is sympathetic to Nora's complaint. "Asians," he says, "are today's

Jews." Stetson's insight is crucial to understanding why many people today want to scrap America's thirty-year-old affirmative action policies. Anyone who looks at the historical pattern of discrimination in admission to elite universities must conclude that Jews have been discriminated against, too. From the 1920s to the late 1940s, Harvard, Yale, and Princeton imposed admissions quotas on Jews; during the same period, Harvard and Yale took on a handful of blacks each year, while Princeton admitted none. And yet while affirmative action policies are intended to redress historical injustices, the policy does not redress the injustice against Jews. Why not? Because Jews pulled themselves up without benefit of federal programs. Asians have done so, too, Stetson argues, and thus it seems to Asian-Americans like Nora and her mom that they are being punished for having succeeded in bettering themselves.

Thomas Kean, head of Drew University and former Governor of New Jersey, says some colleges have "invisible quotas" for Asian-Americans done in the name of "diversity." "Nobody wants to talk about this," he told me in an interview, "but the word is very much around at most highly-selective colleges. People are practicing that discrimination."

I asked Nora whether she would be mad at Alice if Alice lived in a disadvantaged inner-city neighborhood. Under those circumstances, Nora said, Alice would deserve a break. Nora's reply points to another reason why many whites and nonaffirmative action minorities think the present system needs to be overhauled. Like Nora, Alice lived in a very affluent community with a great public high school. Being black hadn't handicapped her by any specific socioeconomic criteria, yet she was the beneficiary of the same advantages as disadvantaged blacks. Why? Because affirmative action is based on race, not on economic class.

"On occasion," wrote Hargadon, "I've looked back and wondered if we might not have avoided some of the divisiveness that results from affirmative action had we taken the economically disadvantaged route. But then part of me says that such a path might well have (indeed, given our history up to the mid-1960s, very likely would have) simply missed the point. My hunch is that affirmative action based on socioeconomic grounds might very well have been carried out without any significant increase in the enrollment of students from Black, Hispanic, or Native American backgrounds. It's pretty clear, I think, that the reasons why students from such minority backgrounds were so rarely to be found in institutions such as Princeton (and Swarthmore and Stanford, the two other schools I've been associated with) prior to the mid-1960s, involved more than simply economic factors. Indeed, at all of our institutions, it is possible to go back many decades and find non-minority students from economically disadvantaged backgrounds—but few, if any, minority students of whatever socioeconomic background. So, after a lot of thought, no, I am just not persuaded that basing our affirmative action efforts on the economically disadvantaged would have been a better path to take then, nor do I think we have yet been so successful in our efforts that it would be wise to change the focus of our affirmative action at this time."

In a similar vein, Hargadon asks himself: "But what about the middle-class Black student from the prep school? Isn't he taking a place that could be filled by a poor Black student?"

His answer was, "First, don't assume that every minority student from a prep school is middle-class or otherwise economically advantaged. Many minority students coming to Princeton and other colleges from independent schools were originally recruited by those schools under *their* affirmative action programs and attended those schools only by virtue of considerable economic assistance. Second, don't make the classic error of assuming that all Black (or Hispanic, or Native American) students are at Princeton only as the direct result of our affirmative action efforts. Third, since we can admit only about one of every six applicants, it could be said that *any* student at Princeton is 'taking the place' of other deserving students. A middle-class Black student is no more 'taking the place' of a poor Black student than is any other enrolled student, middle-class or not, minority or not. Fourth, while we would certainly like to enroll something on the order of a 'critical mass' of minority students at Princeton, we do not set aside a particular number of places in the freshman class for such students, and given the deplorable condition of the schools in which so many minority students across the country find themselves, no institution I am familiar with (including Princeton) has so many qualified minority applicants that it makes sense to think that one Black student, from whatever background, is somehow 'taking the place' of another Black student."

In describing how affirmative action works at Princeton, Hargadon wrote, "For Princeton, affirmative action is largely a matter of our making aggressive efforts to seek out and identify academically qualified students from particular minority backgrounds (Black, Hispanic, and Native American), encouraging them to apply, and then encouraging those to whom we offer admission to enroll. In sum, we try very hard to get such students on our radar screen and to get Princeton on their radar screens. Such efforts include special mailings, targeted school visits, the use of students (Minority Associates), the use of members of our Alumni Schools Committees, contacts with agencies and organizations . . . and the like. And, when assessing a student's academic achievements and abilities and potential for success at Princeton, we also take into consideration any educational disadvantages that may have accrued . . . from a specific minority background. As in the case of every applicant, minority or non-minority, we ask ourselves how well a student has used the (sometimes limited) resources available."

All too often, those resources are very limited. One day at a senior administrative meeting, someone asked why Princeton has so few students from the entire Chicago public school system. Hargadon became defensive, and at the next meeting he had statistics showing how few Chicago students meet the minimum requirements of an elite university. While he personally writes to them and offers admission to many, he said, there are so many prestigious institutions after such a small pool of qualified kids that it is extremely difficult to get a sizable number of them to enroll at Princeton.

Or anywhere else. "Harvard killed us," said Rice's Barry McFarland, when I asked him how Rice had done on enrolling minority students the previous year. McFarland immediately vowed to do unto Harvard as Harvard had done unto Rice.

As Hargadon's and McFarland's frustration suggests, affirmative action has succeeded in increasing minority students' access to elite universities, but it has not increased the number of minority students who are qualified to pass through those doors. As Hargadon put it, "The trickle-down effects have been nowhere near as substantial as we had hoped for."

CHAPTER ▢ **20**

"**N**o center yet."
That was the note Hargadon scribbled on a piece of
scrap paper during a late winter morning meeting with famed
Princeton basketball coach Pete Carril. No young man of
extraordinary height able to shoot and rebound a basketball
had yet been enticed to come to Princeton.

Anyone who follows college basketball knows that over the
last quarter century Carril's cagers have won more than their
share of Ivy League championships and have participated in
several memorable postseason tournament games. Carril's
victories and near-victories (the latter topped by Princeton's
famous last-second loss to Goliath Georgetown) have made
him a revered figure on the Princeton campus. As celebrated a
figure as he is, however, and for all the passion students and
alumni bring to their support for the team, once a suitable
player is found, the coach won't be able to offer the young
man an athletic scholarship or completely guarantee him a
spot in the freshman class.

Such is the conundrum that is sports at Princeton.

A century ago, Princeton and its Ivy brethren were

America's big-time sports universities, tarred by the same suspicions of professionalism and commercialism that other universities are today. In 1889 Princeton and Harvard accused each other of making illicit monetary payments to football players and allowing players to enroll late. In 1885 and 1886 Princeton professors refused to let students play off campus because it was disrupting their studies. Under pressure from students and alumni, the ban was lifted, and the Princeton–Yale Thanksgiving Day football game became again a highlight of the fall social season for Manhattan's elite.

Over time, however, Princeton and the other Ivies reformed their sports programs, so that today they are considered models of how to avoid the excesses of big-time sports. Not only are no athletic scholarships given out, there are no athlete-only dormitories. Furthermore, the athletic department budget is part of, not separate from, the university's general budget. Yet the Ivies have remained a big-time sports fraternity, its members as intent on winning championships as they were a century ago.

In a nutshell, the candidate who is a great athlete—someone who has earned state, regional, or national recognition in a sport—has a huge advantage in the admissions process, while the applicant who is just a very good high school athlete—even the star of his team—does not. When applying to an elite university, a candidate who is also an accomplished athlete needs to know not just whether his or her name appears on a coach's recruiting list but how many other names are on that list and, even more important, *where* his or her name is on that list.

To be sure, being a star athlete won't help a student get into some schools. Reed, for example, doesn't have intercollegiate sports. Many small liberal arts colleges field teams consisting of students who only incidentally happen to be athletes.

But a number of very selective national universities are affiliated with big-time sports leagues. Northwestern, for example, competes against Ohio State, Michigan State, and others, in the Big Ten. Rice goes up against Houston and the University of Texas in the Southwest Conference. Vanderbilt must challenge the universities of Georgia, Alabama, and Tennessee in the Southeastern Conference. While all three have trouble winning against much bigger state schools, Duke is at the top of the heap in the Atlantic Coast Conference, often besting the universities of Maryland, Virginia, and North Carolina. In every sport but football, the Ivies square off against the top-ranked teams in the country. In some sports, they *are* the top-ranked teams.

"Ivy League athletics, in the world of people who read the *New York Daily News*, is not considered to be a high-powered athletic league. But it is," says Bob Myslik, at the time Princeton's athletic director. In fact, "It's probably the most high-powered athletic league, if you exclude the so-called revenue sports, particularly football, where we basically opted out."

If, as Princeton student F. Scott Fitzgerald once said, "the test of a first-rate intelligence is the ability to hold two opposed ideas in the mind at the same time and still retain the ability to function," then the Ivy approach to sports is highly intelligent. On the one hand, Princeton wants to win, and it recruits a significant number of students for that purpose. On the other hand, it believes that a student's athletic ability should be secondary to his or her academic ability.

By trying to fulfill these two basically contradictory objectives, the admissions process ends up seeming unfair to every applicant. According to Myslik, Princeton "historically" admits sixty to seventy percent of the athletes it recruits, confirmation that an applicant with top-ranked athletic ability enjoys an incredible advantage over the nonathletic applicant. From the point of view of the recruited athlete, however, the obvious question is why he or she should have a thirty to forty percent chance of *not* being admitted after having been pursued.

While Pennsylvania admits about one out of three candidates overall, it admits better than one out of two candidates who appear on a coach's recruiting list. For those applicants who are first, second, or third on a coach's list, the chances of being accepted are about ninety percent. (With a greater need for bodies, the football coach gets roughly his top twenty prospects.) Penn's admissions dean, Lee Stetson, emphasizes that the admits are academically qualified. But since roughly eighty to ninety percent of all candidates to elite institutions are "qualified," the athletic advantage at Penn is huge for, as Stetson puts it, "the ones the coaches *really* want."

If the Ivies competed for national championships in only a couple of sports, the recruitment of athletes probably wouldn't be an admissions problem. But the top eastern schools and those other liberal arts colleges who follow the same model of education play more varsity sports than does a big state university. In 1991 Michigan had twenty-one varsity sports while Harvard, Princeton, Yale, Cornell, Pennsylvania, and Dartmouth each had thirty or more. The combination of more sports and smaller student bodies means that recruited athletes at the elite liberal arts colleges constitute a much higher percentage of the student body than at a sports "factory" like Michigan. In 1991 only 1.8 percent of Michigan students participated in varsity sports, compared with 25.2 percent at Princeton.

To be sure, there are "walk-ons" at Ivy schools, particularly in the sports of crew, fencing, and lightweight football. However, "when you have a league that's as good as ours is athletically in Division One, you're not going to rely upon some statistical fallout of admits who happen to wander down to the gym and show up for, [say,] the lacrosse team," Myslik said. In 1992, when the Princeton men's lacrosse team won the national collegiate championship, the coach unabashedly told a press conference that he couldn't have done it without Hargadon.

A freshman class where roughly 20 percent of the students have been recruited for their athletic ability seems antithetical to the primary objective of an elite university, namely, the academic preparation of tomorrow's leaders. When John C. Sawhill, former president of New York University, delivered his valedictory address as a member of Princeton's board of trustees in 1991, he questioned whether Princeton's "pursuit of the scholar-athlete ideal has been detrimental to our academic programs.

"Don't get me wrong," Sawhill said in the faculty room of Nassau Hall, built in the eighteenth century to resemble the British House of Commons. "I'm as much a fan of successful athletic teams as anyone else. But as we've added varsity sport after varsity sport—there are now more than thirty of them—it's possible that the sheer numbers have begun to conspire against the university's greater educational purpose. There are, of course, many exceptional scholar-athletes, but it seems to me that we need to consider the academic consequences of emphasizing physical rather than intellectual qualifications."

Implicit in Sawhill's criticism was the charge that some recruited athletes don't belong at Princeton because their academic credentials are inadequate. Two years after Sawhill's speech, President Shapiro basically conceded that recruited athletes are held to a lower standard when he said in a strategic-planning report that one of the university's "continuing" goals was to improve "the overall academic qualifications that our recruited athletes bring to campus."

Hargadon would say that he "agonized" over some of the recruited athletes he admitted. But John Fleming, the professor of English and comparative literature and Master of Wilson College, took it one step further in admitting, "There are a large number of recruited athletes—now this doesn't account for every recruited athlete by any means—but recruited athletes who, on the whole, are not of the intellectual and academic quality of most of their peers."

And yet as critical as he was, Fleming made an important concession. He conceded that the so-called dumb jocks were "academically adequate" by Princeton's own high standards, meaning that, while some recruited athletes may not be *as* smart as most of their nonathletic peers, they are still the crème de la crème of college-caliber athletes as a group.

"When you talk about the problems of attracting smart athletes, football and basketball are the big bugaboo. You can find smart tennis players and golfers," said Rice's Barry McFarland, adding that once in a great while a particularly gifted athlete who isn't particularly gifted in the classroom will be referred directly to the president of Rice.

Hargadon has reduced the advantage that athletes have in the admissions process at Princeton. According to Myslik, Hargadon cut the number of recruited athletes who are offered admission by shortening the coaches' wish lists. Myslik said that recruiting à la Hargadon is a "rifle shoot," since most coaches can now put together lists of just six to ten kids a year. At Pomona College, there's been a similar transformation. Pomona admissions head Bruce Poch remembers that coaches used to submit lists with hundreds of names on them. Even now, some coaches' lists have fifty names on them; on the day we spoke, Poch complained that the previous year the women's swim team's list had seventy names on it.

The goal, Myslik said, is "fewer but better athletes" for each sport—an approach that puts enormous pressure on coaches to get the students who have been admitted to actually enroll, even while other colleges are dangling athletic scholarships in front of them.

At Princeton, the board of trustees has tried to ease the admissions strain by dropping men's wrestling as a varsity sport and by cutting the target for football recruits from fifty to thirty-five per class, by eliminating freshman football and making freshmen eligible for the varsity. (The football decision was a leaguewide decision, pushed for by Princeton.)

But that still leaves more than thirty varsity sports for a student body of only about 4,500—very nearly the smallest in the Ivy League and likely to stay that way.

The admissions policies of virtually every U.S. college and university, but especially the sports-laden Ivies, could be seriously affected by a lawsuit currently winding its way toward the Supreme Court. In March, 1995, a federal judge found that Brown University was discriminating against its female athletes. Although fifty-one percent to fifty-two percent of Brown's students are women, only about thirty-eight percent of Brown's varsity athletes are female. The judge ordered the university to have the same ratio of male-female athletes as the student body as a whole. Brown officials argued that they already offer virtually every varsity women's sport around— eighteen in all. If Brown loses its case, either the number of varsity women athletes will somehow have to go up, or, more likely, the number of varsity male athletes will have to go down. Football is the big numbers eater; just imagine the hue and cry if Brown has to eliminate its varsity football team!

To be sure, admitting students who have shown a commitment to athletics is desirable. As one high school student-athlete I met put it, "The student who is also an athlete has the ability to spend four hours every single day practicing after school, come home at seven-thirty every night, eat dinner until eight-fifteen, and despite being tired, still do their homework until midnight. . . . It's not whether you're good so much as having the ability to manage your time."

CHAPTER 21

Luck, legacy, affirmative action, athletic prowess—they are all powerful playing cards in college admissions. Yet even in our supposedly egalitarian society there's a fifth card, and it's an ace—money.

Despite all the reforms of the past several decades, there is no denying that having money greatly improves one's chances for admission to a selective school. While it's always been true that the more resources a high school has, the better the preparation it can offer, it's never been more true than it is today that a child's access even to a good public school depends on his parents' bank balance. In his speech to the Princeton Club of Philadelphia, Hargadon said, "If you watch what's happening in secondary education in this country, it is really horrible. When I was growing up, there were many great high schools, whether they were in wealthy areas or not. Now, it really is a have or have-not situation. You get the inner-city schools, which are at the low end, and you get the [great suburban] schools. And there aren't as many in between." In Hargadon's own childhood, rich and poor used to mix more in the same city or town. As poor as his family was,

Hargadon was able to attend very good public schools. It was a system, he says, that served everyone well. "Everybody was held to the same standard."

Hargadon thinks his efforts have produced a broader range of schools represented at Princeton. The number of secondary schools providing the applicant pool increased from 4,666 for the class of 1995 to 5,100 for the class of 1998. The number of schools generally represented in a given class is now roughly nine hundred–plus, compared with eight hundred–plus a few years ago. The dean emphasizes that two consecutive nine hundred–plus classes "could represent two quite different mixes of nine hundred–plus schools. And over four years, the total number of different schools with students at Princeton could change quite significantly. . . ."

The dean doesn't underestimate, however, the inherent advantages that some secondary schools have because they have more money to spend. "Attending a school that has a really rich advanced placement program" is a "tremendous" advantage "in our applicant pool," Hargadon said. "A school that offers all kinds of sports, and good equipment and good coaching and good schedules, gives you an opportunity to do that. Or it's the school that has the money to have an orchestra. It has music teachers. It has fine arts people."

Nor do the advantages of attending a good high school stop there. In Mountain Lakes, New Jersey, where homes sell for half a million dollars and more, there are three full-time guidance counselors for fewer than four hundred high school students—very nearly the optimum counselor-to-student ratio. One year at Mountain Lakes, the admissions head of a selective private college put on a daylong series of workshops:

one for students, one for parents, one for faculty members on letters of recommendation, and one for English teachers on college essay writing.

To be sure, elite universities are forever compensating and making allowances for some applicants' limited academic opportunities. But in explaining why he will reject a valedictorian from one high school, while accepting a candidate who ranked twentieth in his class from another, Hargadon states the undeniable fact that the twentieth-ranked kid often has had a more demanding academic program. "Class rank doesn't mean anything unless you look at the school," Smith College's Ann Wright says flatly.

And the inequity of money doesn't end with questions of quality; it extends to matters of access as well. While there are fifty or so selective and highly selective colleges and universities in America, all but the very top ones must cultivate counselors at America's best high schools in order to ensure that they get the steady stream of outstanding applicants that they want. Each year a group of selective private colleges in California picks up the tab for a weeklong visit by a small group of selected high school counselors from around the United States. Meanwhile, representatives of America's top colleges make sure to drop by the nation's best high schools.

Indeed, one reason why Nancy Siegel of affluent Millburn High School is so successful is that over the years she has gotten to know the admissions people from dozens of institutions. One day, Siegel got on the phone with an admissions person she knew to talk about one of her students who had just been deferred by that university. The admissions person asked Siegel to hold on while she read the student's application. The admissions person then offered some off-the-record advice on what the student should do to improve the chance of being admitted in the spring: changing the academic department the student planned to major in. The student was accepted.

Before Hargadon's day at Princeton, certain school counselors, as well as certain alumni, had tremendous access to Princeton's admissions department. Jim Wickenden was Princeton's admissions head between 1978 and 1983. He remembers that during his tenure certain alumni interviewers influenced the admissions process. "There would be some very, very active alumni who would really do a first-rate job. And when they reached a certain level of frustration, they'd call me at home or call me at the office. And then they would want two more of their kids admitted. And sometimes I would pay attention to them if I knew they were working very hard."

In general, said Wickenden, "if you had two people with the same rating and one came from an area where the Schools Committee was enormously powerful and very aggressive and he or she was on the phone with a regional person [in the admissions office] on a regular basis, the [candidate] from the area where there was an aggressive [alumni] person may get the nod. Most often did."

Some school counselors intervened in the same way, Wickenden remembers. Counselors from upward of twenty private prep schools would trek to Princeton each year and go over their lists of Princeton applicants with the admissions staffer in charge of the region. As often as not, Wickenden says, these prep counselors would lobby on behalf of one or

218 ☐ BILL PAUL

more of their students whom Princeton was disinclined to admit. Then the regional person would go to Wickenden and say something like, "We really should take another look at so-and-so," which Wickenden says he sometimes did.

Since Hargadon arrived, Nancy Siegel says, the lines of communication between Millburn and Princeton have been cut. Indeed, Hargadon has gone so far in the opposite direction from Wickenden that when a professional college counselor called to ask if a blank Princeton application might be mailed to her, the counselor was told no. Princeton's alumni interviewers have been told that their job is to spot strong applicants and to encourage them to come to Princeton—and nothing more.

Even the affluent, however, suffer from a problem in the admissions process: the problem of multiple applications. As it has become statistically more difficult to get into an elite university, young people quite naturally have applied to more of them. Whereas a generation ago a bright high school senior might apply to three or four institutions, today's top seniors apply to seven or eight, nearly all of them selective or highly selective, with a so-called safety school thrown in. The problem with multiple applications is that it is impossible for the admissions department of an elite university to know which university is the student's first choice. You can't ask an applicant which school is his first choice, Hargadon says, because that puts pressure on the kid to tell every school that it is his first choice. Not knowing where applicants really want to go leads each selective university to offer admission to many applicants for whom that university is only their second or third choice. For every student that a school like Princeton offers to admit, it has no choice but to turn down five or six other applicants, some of whom are deserving of a spot in the next freshman class. Sadly, sometimes Princeton rejects deserving students for whom Princeton is the first choice, in favor of candidates who have no intention of going to Princeton if they are also accepted by, say, Harvard or Stanford.

CHAPTER 22

As Hargadon and his staff geared up for the final frantic stretch to the April deadline, one candidate was still in the running whom I felt had the makings of a great Princeton undergrad.

Mark Ghani had a schoolteacher who moonlighted as a guitarist and singer. Knowing that Mark played the violin, the teacher asked him to join his musical group, which Mark did. But in short order, Mark was flying solo, playing his violin for the Friday-night patrons of a coffeehouse where the brightest light in the house was the recessed bulb from the pastry display case. He was the club's featured performer—the guy whose name was on the poster-size marquee—mixing jazz and classical in an improvisational performance that got the hip young crowd that frequented the club on its feet clapping and calling out requests. Mark was obliging, but he drew the line at certain requests, primarily "Phantom of the Opera." While he never took a drink, he never refused the phone number of any attractive young lady who admired his musicianship.

Perhaps coincidentally, perhaps not, Mark also was growing academically. He became active in his school debate club and quickly discovered he was very good. Not just the best in his school, but the best in his region. He was good enough, in fact, to qualify for a national competition, which he did on the basis of his victory in a debate on, of all things, affirmative action.

As Mark later recounted, about halfway through the debate, a resolution was introduced to the effect that affirmative action has been a failure. After a couple of speakers had their say, a girl stood up and argued for five minutes that affirmative action has indeed been a failure. At the end she emphatically declared, "As Lenin once said, 'The road to hell is paved with good intentions.' "

With the crowd still applauding, Mark's name was called out next. With his fists clenched, he began by stating, "This argument has taken the wrong course." He looked down at his hastily written notes, then decided that, as with his violin playing at the jazz club, he would improvise.

"A hundred years ago," he intoned, "a black man could not go to Harvard. People today may complain that affirmative action isn't working. But things *have* changed drastically." He then went on to quote someone by the name of David Ames, whom Mark described as a noted clinical psychologist. As a few kids in the crowd snickered, Mark quoted Ames: "Educational integration has been shown to widen one's world view and make people more open to new ideas." Mark closed by declaring triumphantly, "If the road to hell is paved with good intentions, then send me to hell."

With the judges smiling and the audience roaring, Mark took his seat with other participants from his school. Only they knew that the "noted" clinical psychologist David Ames was actually David Ames their classmate. The entire quote had been fabricated.

Nevertheless, at the end of the day, the judges made Mark their winner, and he took home a statue more than three feet high.

While Mark sent in his Princeton application before much of this growth had occurred, he was still able to tell Hargadon about his new senior-year activities on a separate form that Princeton asks candidates to fill out so that the admissions department can find out what the candidates have been up to since the closing date.

Mark's senior year suggested a young man who, for all he had accomplished so far, was still just beginning to tap his potential. In addition, just like the young woman who raced in demolition derbies, a boy who played classical violin in a coffeehouse likely would have a slightly different way of thinking and looking at the world.

▯ ▯ ▯ ▮ ▯

While Mark grew as a person, Hargadon was going through the same old hell, most of it of his own making. If the dean hadn't had a widely known deadline to meet, he might never have stopped fussing over the mountain of applications. "I hate to let go," he said. As the clock ticked down and secretaries stood by, waiting to stuff and address envelopes, some candidates' folders went first into the admit file, then into the reject file, then back into the admit file, or vice versa.

Hargadon was guilty of the same crime he said everyone else was: he wanted to admit more candidates than he could. And he just might have taken them all, if he had thought he could get away with stuffing four freshmen into a dorm room that was already a squeeze for two.

Well, maybe not all of them. "What do you do when you get a folder of a young woman who's got good grades and test scores and claims to want to major in science, but the thing is they don't have a single test score in math or science other than the math SAT?" the dean plaintively asked. "There is nothing in the folder to suggest that that person will head toward science. No advance placement. Nothing in science. Pretty clearly they decided that their chances would be better as women if they said they're interested in science. I'm sure they read somewhere that colleges are looking for women in science."

For others, Hargadon said, the fatal flaw was being born with a silver spoon in their mouths. They had done well in school but, given all the advantages they had had, no better than what could have been expected. Some advantaged candidates did themselves in by coming across as blasé, as if they felt they were owed a spot in Princeton's next class.

And a few run into trouble with the "recommendations" of Princeton professors. About one applicant's musical tape, a professor in the music department commented, "Sounds like a cat caught in a hot motor."

▯ ▯ ▯ ▮ ▯

The final committee meeting lasted roughly two weeks and took place mostly in Hargadon's office, with the dean and his two top lieutenants in attendance. It went on even as some of next year's applicants were already parading through the outer reception area, picking up admissions brochures. As the number of available places dwindled down to a precious few,

Hargadon or one of his aides would say about this or that applicant, "Haven't seen one like this in a long time," or words to that effect, which indicated that the applicant's chances were good. "What really wears me down," the dean says, "is trying to distinguish between candidates all of whom are really excellent."

As they had during the early action period, the achievements of some candidates, both in and out of the classroom, humbled the dean. Not least were those who had had to overcome grossly unfair conditions. Some candidates jumped out of their folders primarily as fresh, original thinkers and doers. Some clearly would meet many of the needs of the university community.

Others were some or all of the above but not quite as accomplished, or not quite as trailblazing, as the very top group. Many were still in the running—still "swimming" in the pool—in part because, on top of their academic and other achievements, they came across as very likable. Hargadon felt he already knew them because of the "conversations" he'd had with them through their applications. They seemed like kids who'd "fish in the bookstore"; kids who could live, work, and play together; kids who would gain from sharing a common experience, while imparting their own unique slant on life to their fellow students.

Like a soldier with a lot of fight left in him but who has heard the trumpet call to retreat, Hargadon wanted to reach out at least to some whom he personally liked but who were not sufficiently prepared for Princeton. When he was at Stanford, he had been able to admit candidates he called "chances"—kids whose credentials maybe didn't measure up but who he instinctively felt would blossom as they matured. These were the students whose loss he now mourned. At Princeton, there was literally no room to take chances.

Though Princeton never admits more than a handful of applicants from the wait list, Hargadon wait-lists three hundred to four hundred applicants each year. While such a long list may falsely raise some applicants' hopes of still being accepted, the list is long because Hargadon feels that so many candidates deserve better than a letter of rejection. Being wait-listed is "as close as we can come to saying, 'We should have admitted you.' "

So who was getting in now? More than six hundred candidates had been admitted the previous fall. Many early admits had come from superior private or public schools, whose counselors had the background and the time to help students organize their application materials before many other college-bound students in America had even started to think seriously about where to apply. While some athletes had been admitted in the fall, most were taken in the spring, in part because coaches recruited throughout the year. In all, recruited athletes took up more than three hundred spots. Thus, between the fall admitees and the recruited athletes, roughly half the total available spots were already filled.

Another thirty percent or so of total admits were either black, Hispanic, Asian-American, or Native-American—with Asian-Americans slightly above ten percent of total admits, blacks slightly below, and Hispanics at just under eight percent. (Ten Native American applicants were admitted.) Even with the usual overlap, this meant that 1,400 to 1,500 of the approximately two thousand available spaces were now filled.

Foreign students made up another five percent or so of total admits, and the legacy applicants were roughly ten percent, though many of those were already included in these other statistical categories.

Clearly the number of still-available spots had dwindled down to a precious few. It wasn't hard to imagine that at least two of my remaining kids were still on the outside looking in. Both Lucy Simmons and Sirrka Romanski had to rank as long shots, even though both had been first in their class in freshman, sophomore, and junior year. They just didn't stand out amongst the "vast array of stars," to use Shapiro's phrase. Lucy had her math prizes, but she didn't have college credits, and she hadn't attended a top-notch high school. While she had participated in many extracurricular activities, she hadn't put her personal stamp on any of them. Nor did she have a savvy academic counselor. At least with Sirrka, I could imagine a scenario in which, thanks to the letter of recommendation written by her counselor, she would stand out as a unique candidate who would add a new tile to the mosaic. Whatever the reaction to Sirrka's application, one thing that Hargadon would *not* be saying was, "Oh, not another candidate who speaks fluent Serbo-Croatian!"

Although neither Nora Simeon nor Mark Ghani had ever ranked first in their class, I felt better about their chances. While I still thought Nora had made a mess of her application, her academic record was twenty-four-carat gold. Moreover, Nora had put her personal stamp on her school's environmental club. As for Mark, while his academic record wasn't quite as solid, he had excelled in everything but math (which, by the way, he hadn't done badly in). Plus, you had to love a kid who played classical violin in a coffeehouse while winning debate competitions and gaining national musical recognition. Mark would help meet certain specific needs of the Princeton community—assuming, of course, that Lady Luck hadn't intervened and infused the campus with scads of accomplished violinists.

Compared with those whom Hargadon said were the "real" competition, however, neither Nora or Mark seemed all that outstanding. Mark wasn't a musician with a CD. Nora wasn't on the board of an international environmental organization. Neither had been *the* best student whom their teachers or guidance counselors had seen in the last ten or twenty years (and even that accolade didn't make an applicant unique in Princeton's applicant pool). Had they really accomplished enough, with the relatively ample resources available to them, to impress a dean who by his own admission was "really spoiled"?

I reread what Hargadon had written about some of the kids he had admitted the previous year, kids like the demolition derby woman. Come next September, the list of new freshmen would go out to alumni interviewers. The list would reflect the exceedingly high level of individual accomplishment that Princeton expects, not just in the classroom, but in the arts, in sports, and in other leadership positions. It would especially reflect the wide variety of objectives Hargadon seeks to meet, if not every year (applicants, he says, are like "crops," in that they don't all come in every year), then as often as possible. He would begin his letter to us by saying, "While each [new freshman] seems special in his or her own right, those whose outside recognition before they entered Princeton made them particularly visible would include the following:

- eleven Presidential Scholars (second only to a certain university in Cambridge, Mass.)
- four National Science Foundation Young Scholars
- four National Endowment for the Humanities Young Scholars
- the winner of the Moscow Math Olympiad (a Moscow resident)
- the winner of (a prior year's) Moscow Math Olympiad (who had immigrated to New Jersey the year before)
- the silver medalist in the International Math Olympiad
- seven Tandy Technology Scholars (out of one hundred nationally)
- a winner of the California Young Playwright's Contest
- a young woman who had authored and illustrated a children's book
- the National Director of High School Operations for the Rain Forest Conservancy
- four high school Academic All-American rowers and three honorable mentions
- three of the eight National Mars AAU Scholarship winners, selected on the basis of combined academic, athletic, and community service achievements
- a number of musicians whose talents have been recognized at state, regional, and national levels
- Junior Olympic, All-American, and All-State athletes in virtually all men's and women's sports

The final committee meeting ended. The letters went in the mail. "My" kids were about to learn their fate.

CHAPTER ☐ **23**

With the letters from Princeton and the other elite institutions due to arrive in a day or two, Nancy Siegel was in the kitchen area of the Millburn guidance office pouring herself an extra-big cup of coffee. Only half-kiddingly she said, "It's time to get out the rope and tape."

Rope to tie up some of the parents. Tape to keep their mouths shut.

Siegel had spent the morning trying to restrain several parents from calling various colleges to find out whether their kids had been accepted. "They're so out of their minds with worry that they don't see how foolish they would look," she said. "Who knows?" she added. "Even at this point, a call like that might screw things up for the kid."

Then there were the parents who didn't want to talk to a university but to Siegel—not once but, in some cases, over and over, day after day, sometimes more than once a day. "I'd be good as a crisis counselor on a hotline," she said, smiling. Then, before she could swallow her first taste of coffee, the phone rang.

She picked it up, then said into the receiver, "Yes, how are you?" Looking over at me, she mouthed the words, "Here's another one."

"Yes, I know how nerve-wracking it can be. I'm not looking forward to it when my kids apply to college."

The mother at the other end of the line then talked for a full two minutes while Siegel doodled on a note pad and said "uh-huh" several times. Finally Siegel said, "Look on the bright side. At least it's almost over."

Apparently that did not have the desired effect of calming this mother and getting her off the phone. "Look," Siegel quickly added, "the bell is about to ring, and in a minute or two my office is going to be wall-to-wall kids. Call me back if you need to, but really, just try to relax, okay?"

When the kids piled into her office, Siegel, despite the maelstrom, seemed almost relieved. After helping a sophomore with a scheduling change, she turned to me and said, "At least that's a problem I can do something about."

Then a senior burst in, looking as if someone had died. "Is it true?" she shrieked.

"Is what true?" Siegel asked, deeply concerned.

"Is it true that the letters from Penn are going to be late?"

Siegel felt like screaming, How the hell should I know? Instead, she quietly said, "Would you like me to call them and find out?"

"Oh, would you? Please," the girl entreated. You'd think she was begging for her life.

"When I get the chance," Siegel said.

"Oh, please. Now?"

Siegel put her head in her hands. "All right," she said, then picked up the receiver. She turned to me. "If I don't call, there'll be a hundred Millburn students calling the Penn admissions office. Think how that would look."

□ □ □ ▮ □

Sirrka couldn't wait for her letter to come in the mail, and since she was already on the Princeton campus attending a class, she didn't have to. She walked over to West College, past Nassau Hall and the Revolutionary War cannon and the century-old dormitories, any one of which she prayed she would be in come September. She told the receptionist that she was an applicant and asked what the decision on her had been. When she was told, she quietly walked back outside.

She had been rejected—again, and this time it was for good. She walked around for a while before heading back to her high school. Later, when she got home from ballet class, the letter from Princeton was waiting for her. She opened it and reacted once again with the same stoic calm.

□ □ □ ▮ □

When her Princeton letter came, Lucy did the same thing she had done in the fall. She raced home after the final school bell, took the mail out of the mailbox, and sat down alone in her house. She opened the other mail before she opened the letter from Princeton. It was the thin envelope she had dreaded all along, but when she read it, she didn't break down in tears. She did, however, scoop up another bowl of ice cream in which to drown her sorrows.

□ □ □ ▮ □

The postman delivered Nora's mail on Saturday around midday. The letter from Princeton was one of four responses she got that day. (Only Yale's wasn't included in the bunch.) She decided to open the Princeton letter last. The first letter was an acceptance. The second letter was an acceptance. The third letter was an acceptance. The fourth and final letter was—a rejection. As much as she had feared it, Nora still couldn't believe that Princeton had said no.

▢　▢　▢　❚　▢

Mark's letter arrived on a Friday, but he didn't see it until late that night when he returned from a date with his girlfriend. When he walked in the door, his parents were in bed and the Princeton letter was on the mantel in the living room. It had been a good night, and when Mark saw the letter, he froze, afraid that the evening was about to be ruined. He looked at his girlfriend, took a very deep breath, and slit open the envelope.

"Yes!" the letter began.

"Yes!" Mark shouted.

Mark did a somersault in the middle of the living room. Then he did another. And another. And another.

CONCLUSION

After the letters left his office, bound for mailboxes all over the world, Hargadon felt he had to get away from it all, at least for a little while. So he took a train to New York City, where he visited some museums. He also stopped by Brooks Brothers and bought a shirt. When he handed his credit card to the saleswoman, she looked at it closely. "Are you the Fred Hargadon at Princeton?" she asked.

"Yes, I am," he said.

The woman burst into tears. Princeton, she told him, had just rejected her daughter.

The reactions of other parents, students, and supporters of rejected candidates were less dramatic but no less heart-felt.

Rejected by Princeton but accepted by Wellesley and Amherst, as well as William and Mary, Nora still didn't appreciate how well she had done. Sitting in her living room, she complained about the unfairness of the Princeton system. What galled her was that another student in her high school class had gotten in, despite having lower grades and test scores than hers. In Nora's mind, there was only one possible explanation: she had been passed over in favor of a lightweight legacy, a less-qualified kid—whose father had gone to Princeton.

A couple of weeks later, I telephoned Nora to see where she had decided to go. She said that all the kids in her high school had been telling her she should go to Wellesley.

"Why?" I asked.

"Because they think that Wellesley has a better reputation and that I'm going to need that reputation after I graduate."

"But what do you *want* to do?" I asked.

"I had a hard time deciding, but I'm going to go to Amherst."

"The school you liked from the very beginning, right?"

"Uh-huh."

"Are you happy with your choice?"

"I think so," she said.

▯ ▯ ▯ ▮ ▯

Lucy had been rejected not only by Princeton but by Harvard and Yale. She went out with her boyfriend and partied hard to forget, almost overlooking the fact that she had been accepted at Duke. But even though she felt dejected at first, Lucy, unlike Nora, bounced back quickly. Three days after she learned she would be going to Duke in the fall, Duke won the men's national basketball championship.

Before the rejection letters arrived, Lucy hadn't paid any attention to the kids in school walking around in Michigan sweatshirts in anticipation of the favored Wolverines defeating the Blue Devils in the NCAA title game. But when she got dressed for school that morning, she decided, for the heck of it, to wear a Duke sweatshirt. When she ran into a pack of Michigan rooters, she found herself saying, "*We* kicked your butt last night."

That was the moment it really hit her that the long process was finally over. She hadn't gotten into either her first-, second-, or even her third-choice college, but suddenly it didn't matter. It felt good to be a Blue Devil.

"Would being a Princeton Tiger have been better?" I later asked.

She thought for a moment. "Well, I'm not. It's time to move on."

One reason Lucy recovered quickly was that she had always thought of herself as a long shot at Harvard, Princeton, and Yale. Also, Duke hadn't just accepted her—it had recognized her academic achievement by giving her advanced standing in chemistry.

▯ ▯ ▯ ▮ ▯

Princeton, the college love of her life, had jilted her, but Sirrka too bounced back quickly. She told me over the phone that the first thing she had done was look through the catalogs of the colleges that had accepted her, among them two excellent institutions: Pennsylvania and Johns Hopkins. In doing so, she had rediscovered why she had applied to Penn. "I want to be a doctor, and Penn has all these premed courses I want to take."

"Does Princeton have the same courses?" I asked.

"No," she said, surprised at her own answer. She thought for a moment, then said, "Penn's courses were always appealing, but I wouldn't let myself like them."

"Sounds like Penn is the right match for you," I said.

"Definitely," she said.

□ □ □ ▮ □

Even though Mark Ghani had gotten into Princeton, he had been rejected again by his first-choice school, Harvard. Still, returning to the plus side, he had gotten into Stanford as well, leaving him feeling like the double-winner he was. But now he had to decide which university to attend. When he visited the Stanford campus in Palo Alto, the students he met seemed more interested in talking him *out* of going to Princeton than in talking him *into* going to Stanford. Many of the Stanford students he talked to, he discovered, had been rejected by Princeton. Still, it wasn't until Mark visited the Princeton campus that he made his decision. The picture he had had in his mind of New Jersey as an ugly place simply did not apply, and he liked the students he met and the classes he sat in on. Mark had the luxury of doing things his own way: He could decide which college was the best match for him after the admissions process was over.

Josh Hastings was also in that enviable position. Like Mark, Josh could choose either Princeton or Stanford, the two schools that had started out as his co-first choices because each had a strong liberal arts program wrapped around a great engineering school. Unlike Mark, Josh made up his mind very quickly. He decided to attend Princeton because, as he put it, he had been thinking of himself as a Princeton undergraduate since being admitted way back in December. Also, like a majority of all college students, Josh wanted to go to an institution that was close to home.

☐ ☐ ☐ ▮ ☐

At the Princeton admissions office, letters from the disappointed were flooding in. Hargadon's secretary stacked them on her boss's desk. Each boiled down to a single irate question: "How could you?!" As in: How could you reject my child, my grandchild, my student, my former student, my counselee, my neighbor's kid? Each writer came at it with his own ax to grind. So-and-so should have been accepted because: his or her grades were so good; test scores so high; recommendations so fine; was so highly accomplished in this skill or that activity; had overcome a disadvantaged background; and on and on.

"Everyone has his own definition of merit," said Hargadon.

Still, the dean was not without sympathy. In general, his written responses to these letters had a comforting tone.

There was nothing wrong with the candidate, he would say, and Princeton would have loved to have him or her, if only there were more room.

Some correspondents, however, felt Hargadon's sharp tongue. One complaining letter from a parent noted that the son had been admitted to Harvard, MIT, Dartmouth, Cornell, the University of Chicago, and others. The parent's line of reasoning was that these other acceptances proved that the young man should also have been accepted by Princeton. Hargadon wrote back that the boy was "fortunate" that while he could attend only one college in the fall, he had seven very good ones to choose from.

Nor did Hargadon have much sympathy for rejected legacy candidates—not when over 40 percent of them were accepted. By chance, he had run into a member of the university's board of trustees on a sidewalk on the campus. The trustee remarked that several of his alumni friends had been complaining that their children or their friends' children had been rejected. He asked Hargadon how he could politely get them off his back. Hargadon told the trustee to tell his friends that at some point showing too much preference for alumni children could jeopardize the university's tax-exempt status. Tell them, Hargadon suggested, that Uncle Sam might think Princeton was using its status as a public-interest, tax-exempt institution to feather its own nest. The trustee saw Hargadon's logic and thanked him for his advice. "After all these years," Hargadon said to me, "I'm surprised I didn't think of that until just now."

In our last meeting, Hargadon told me that when he retires, he would like to write a mystery built around a college admissions department, also, maybe, the lyrics to a musical comedy. But he was in no rush to pack up. "If I'd thought I'd gotten it perfect, I would retire," he said. "But I don't think I've gotten it right yet. The one person you don't want as dean of admissions is the person who thinks they have it down pat."

☐ ☐ ☐ ▌ ☐

As the school year drew to a close, I read a book that Hargadon requires all his staffers to read. The author is John W. Gardner, founder of the public interest group Common Cause, and its title, *Excellence—Can We Be Equal and Excellent, Too?* poses the question that is at the heart of the challenge facing American education as we approach the twenty-first century—a time when man's principal working tool will be his mind, and society's main product will be information.

Hargadon wants his staffers to read *Excellence* because the book, he believes, captures the inherent difficulty of choosing the "best" students for the best universities. Americans have always had two, partially contradictory notions of what is fair, Gardner states. On the one hand, we believe that everyone should rise or fall on his or her own merits, and may the best man win. On the other hand, we believe that everyone should have an equal opportunity to succeed, a level playing field on which to start life. For Hargadon, the "best" students, the ones most deserving of admission, are those who make the most of the opportunities they have, both in and out of the classroom. Unfortunately, Hargadon, no more than any other dean of admissions at a selective university, has no way to compensate fully for the fact that some young people have fewer opportunities than others.

Still, it should not be the job of a dean of admissions to create a level playing field. That's the job of society itself—of public primary and secondary schools, parents, and whole communities. In the end, it shouldn't matter whether a young person gets into Princeton or Paducah State, or goes directly from high school into the work force. The only thing that should matter is whether that young person is a "first-rate human being," able to feel and eager to learn. Hargadon used the phrase "first-rate human being" in an article he wrote for the Princeton Class of 1926, reprinted in Princeton's alumni magazine in 1991. When the '26ers had asked him how they could get their grandchildren into Princeton, Hargadon replied by telling them how to make their grandkids "C"

children—children with the attributes of citizenship, competence, confidence, character, curiosity, compassion, crafts-
manship, and colleagueship. Hargadon's article, along with
the writings of some of the foremost reformers and observers
of American education, provides a blueprint for answering
Gardner's poignant question in the affirmative.

Ironically, at a time when parents, educators—all of
society—is obsessed with technological gizmos, Hargadon
writes, "If I were limited to one piece of advice . . . I'd tell
[children] to read, read, read. . . . Of all the activities our
children and grandchildren can engage in, reading seems to
me the most enabling one of all."

In 1976, before the computer age took hold, Terrell H.
Bell wrote *Active Parent Concern*, a book on how parents can
help their children do better in school. He opened the book
by declaring, "Parents should demonstrate commitment to
education by establishing a home in which learning is empha-
sized. Books, magazines, and reading material should sur-
round the child during the growing years."

In recent years officials at Millburn High School have
put a great deal of emphasis on computers. But the forma-
tion of a new student group called Bibliophiles has gone
largely unnoticed by administrators and the community at
large. The group grew out of a casual conversation between
a student and his English teacher about how other books
each had read connected in some way to a text the whole
class was reading. In its first year, Bibliophiles had half a
dozen or so members and met several times to discuss books.
But as the club members lobbied for which books would be
picked for discussion, they had one-to-one discussions with

each other that led them to read several other books on their own.

"We sell each other. We sell our authors," one group member explained to me at a meeting in May in the Millburn guidance room. When I asked one girl why she joined the group, she remarked, "I read for the joy of reading. We all do."

"My author is J. R. R. Tolkien," one young man said. "I've read *Lord of the Rings* nine times. Everyone thinks I'm crazy, but there are different ways to read it, different meanings you can get out of it."

A reading club can be beneficial even for kids too young to read. Margaret Greer, the Princeton professor who said Hargadon looks for students who learn for learning's sake, fondly recalls that when her own two children were very young, she and another mother regularly read nursery rhymes to a group of children, then stirred their imaginations by having them think of alternative endings to the stories. "You'd be amazed," she said, laughing, "how many endings you can think of to *Jack and the Beanstalk*." Greer's method of early academic enrichment appears to have worked. When we spoke, she was the mom of a Princeton undergraduate.

▫ ▫ ▫ ▮ ▫

The second piece of advice Hargadon gives is that, "at the earliest stage possible, [children] should begin to learn a second language. There really is no reason why our children should not be bilingual by the time they graduate from high school (as are many of their peers in other countries). Theirs will be an even more international life than has been that of their parents or grandparents. Indeed, I'd go even farther, and wherever possible I'd opt for having them spend at least one of their high school years abroad, an experience that would enable them to more fully appreciate their own culture as well as that of others and at the same time to begin to develop their independence."

Educators often invoke the notion of a rapidly shrinking world, to justify having more foreign students on a college campus. But as Mark Mullin, headmaster of St. Albans School, points out in his 1991 book, *Educating for the 21st Century—The Challenge for Parents and Teachers*: "Just as the students of the 1990s must be educated to interact with the diverse cultures of the world, they must also be prepared for a very different cultural life in America." Gone, Mullin says, are the days when Americans "shared a common language, a common American dream, and a common vision of what America meant." Today there are several American "cultures," including a black culture, an Hispanic culture, a Muslim culture, and a white religious fundamentalist culture.

So one needn't leave the United States to go "abroad," as Hargadon encourages young people to do. One has only to go to the next town or county. At two northern New Jersey high schools—Mountain Lakes High School and John F. Kennedy High—I discovered kids who had journeyed to foreign countries just by going to each other's schools.

Mountain Lakes kids grow up in large, luxurious homes, many of them on lakefront property. For decades their pristine suburban community openly practiced racial and ethnic discrimination. Today, more than ninety percent of Mountain Lakes residents remain white. Kennedy kids, on the other hand, grow up in the racially mixed inner city of Paterson, a city that never recovered economically from the riots of the late 1960s; where being Hispanic can mean you are Puerto Rican, Mexican, Colombian, or none of the above; and where African-Americans and Hispanics have their own difficulties getting along.

One May afternoon, Kennedy and Mountain Lakes kids met in the spacious auditorium of Mountain Lakes High School. (Earlier, the Mountain Lakes kids had journeyed to Paterson.) After wolfing down the universal teenage luncheon of pizza and soft drinks, the young people set up their chairs in a circle. Of the two dozen there, only three were boys. All the Paterson kids were black or Hispanic, and all the Mountain Lakes students were white.

The topic of discussion was an article that had just appeared in *The New York Times*, about how more and more Americans are retreating behind the walls of self-contained communities that invariably are all-white. The group's joint founders and advisers—one a Mountain Lakes assistant principal, the other a J.F.K. history teacher—opened the discussion by asking the group members what they thought about this trend.

"They're just trying to keep people like me out," said one of the Paterson kids.

After that, things quickly got personal, yet the atmosphere in the room did not grow tense. On the contrary, it was almost like that of a church confessional. One girl from Mountain Lakes apologetically described how, as a small child, she had shaken hands with a black woman, then looked at her hand and said to her mother, "Mommy, it won't come off."

A girl from Paterson admitted that there are nonwhite racists and said she would be as uneasy living in a one-race community as whites seemed to be with living in a multiracial one. "We're both just doing what we are familiar with," she said.

One J.F.K. senior whose family had emigrated from Colombia said everyone should admit that if they weren't in this room but were passing one another on the street, they'd go "uh-oh" and turn away.

▢ ▢ ▢ ▮ ▢

The third piece of advice Hargadon has for parents and grandparents is to "introduce [children] to a wide variety of activities or hobbies, letting them settle into the ones that truly engage their interest and abilities, be they in music or art or athletics or any number of areas that would enable them to enjoy themselves, to develop their talents, and to gain a sense of both competence and confidence." In doing so they will more likely bring up a creative child. As psychologist Teresa M. Amabile puts it in her 1989 book, *Growing Up Creative*: "The creativity intersection is the area where your child's *skills* and *interests* overlap. It is the place where your child is most likely to be creative. You can help your children discover their own deepest interests by encouraging them to try out a variety of activities. Present opportunities in low-key ways, then sit back and watch your kids take off."

Clearly, following through on each of Hargadon's three pieces of advice—reading voraciously, learning other languages and cultures, and trying out different hobbies and activities—does not require a lot of money. Indeed, as long as there is a public library nearby, being poor is no handicap to doing the most "enabling" activity of all—reading.

Still, to grow up a "first-rate human being," Hargadon writes, it helps to have a little luck. In a passage reminiscent of his own childhood, he observes that "the luckiest young men and women are those who while growing up benefitted from the contributions to their lives made by what I have come to call 'significant other adults'; a teacher, a neighbor who hires us to mow his lawn, a favorite aunt or uncle, or a coach. For the luckiest of all, perhaps, the most significant of 'significant other adults' are one's grandparents, . . . [who] are in the best position to take the long view and to keep things in perspective."

In his 1991 book, *Smart Schools, Smart Kids,* noted education writer Edward B. Fiske describes in detail what is known in the educational community as the Comer model or the Comer process. It "starts with the assumption that . . . human beings thrive in supportive environments," writes Fiske. Comer is James P. Comer, a Yale psychiatrist who serves on the staff of that university's Child Study Center. Having grown up poor and black in East Chicago, Indiana, Comer told Fiske, he had succeeded in life because the adults he had known as a child had been "locked into a conspiracy to see that I grew up a responsible person." This experience he transformed into the Comer process, a way of educating that involves a great many "significant other adults" in a child's life.

According to Betty Young-Barkley, a liaison between a student's home and school and other community agencies at a Comer model school in Landover, Maryland, "The difference with Comer is that he has involved the parents more and has said that there are significant others in a child's life who should be consulted and involved. . . . Everybody who can be of assistance should be of assistance. . . . If a kid relates to a custodian, we involve the custodian. Whoever the kid relates to, that is what is important."

As Fiske points out, naturally supportive environments like the kind the Comer process is meant to create are becoming rare in America. "Before World War II," Fiske writes, "when the United States was a nation of small towns and rural areas, there was plenty of interaction between children and adults. Youngsters saw adults at work and in their neighborhoods, and young and old alike had a sense of belonging."

In the theories of two of America's most respected education reformers, Howard Gardner of Harvard and Theodore Sizer of the Coalition of Essential Schools at Brown, this idea of a supportive environment, of a conspiracy of significant others working together to help a young person become a first-rate human being, underlies the teaching revolution that they and others are trying to foment.

The old method of teaching, the one most of today's adults grew up with, took hold in the nineteenth century. The assumption was that a child's mind was, to use a Sizer phrase, an "empty slate" and that it was the teacher's job to "imprint" on that mind. Thus teachers lectured, and students recycled that information on multiple-choice tests. This philosophy was a natural fit for an age when America was rapidly becoming professionalized and technologized. After all, to become a doctor or an assembly-line worker requires having a set of facts and figures imprinted on one's mind.

But as Fiske points out, "the 'thinking society' of the twenty-first century can no longer be content with graduates trained to take in and recycle information. . . . Today's students must be taught to think for themselves and to generate new information."

The new method of learning, the so-called *active* learning method, relies on a conspiracy of significant others to help students learn how to think for themselves. Gardner talks about the importance of utilizing community resources, of having young children participate in the highly interactive programs at children's museums, of having skilled craftsmen work with older children in a master-to-apprentice relationship—all in order to indoctrinate children in the "project way of life." Sizer emphasizes children teaching one another by working together in small groups, as well as with teachers, to produce a variety of "portfolios" of work, which are reviewed by still other teachers and school officials and by their parents. In compiling a portfolio, a child learns the three Rs, not for their own sake as under the old method but as a language for thinking and creating. Portfolios are multidimensional, containing elements of writing, public speaking, music and art appreciation, and more. They are rooted in real world role-playing. For example, one of Sizer's suggested science tests (or "exhibitions," as he refers to them) calls for students to act as their school's nutritionist and design lunch menus that are both nutritional and attractive, while staying within a prescribed budget. The students must publicly defend their choices, marshal information, read and write, apply scientific and mathematical concepts, conduct scholarly research, and so on. Then the school votes to determine the "winning" menus.

If and when the new teaching methods espoused by

Gardner, Sizer, and other reformers becomes the standard in American primary and secondary education, something truly remarkable may happen: namely, America's children just may become equal and excellent, too. Just as it doesn't take a lot of money for a parent or grandparent to act on Hargadon's three pieces of advice, it doesn't take a lot of money for a school to implement this new-style curriculum. (It's a lot cheaper to make the school nutritionist part of a conspiracy of significant others than it is to equip a school with new computers and textbooks.) Moreover, as Fiske notes, if and when this curriculum becomes the norm in American education, many of the advantages currently enjoyed by the nation's most affluent public schools may disappear. "The residents of well-to-do areas like Scarsdale, New Trier, and Beverly Hills tend to be satisfied with the quality of their schools—and why not? Their students routinely rack up the best standardized test scores in their respective states, and graduates successfully compete for places in the best colleges and universities," notes Fiske, adding that the new curriculum will expose the weaknesses of these schools in terms of their ability to actually teach students how to think for themselves. Fiske: "The satisfaction that parents in Wilmette enjoy knowing that their children do far better than those on the south side of Chicago is likely to be quickly dissipated by documentation that some still cannot string together a series of coherent paragraphs."

America's elite colleges and universities are in a position to take some responsibility for secondary educational reform. There are few, if any, more prosperous "communities" of Americans than the graduates of America's elite schools. Currently, elite institutions see their alumni simply as sources of money. But if colleges and universities were to link the legacy preference that their alumni enjoy in the admissions process with a binding commitment by alumni to roll up their sleeves and work with young people, the community of significant others conspiring to help young people grow up to be first-rate human beings would be extended.

Every college and university, not just the prestigious ones, can help bring about this revolution by working with the growing number of reform-minded schools and educators all over the United States. Indeed, it is in the colleges' own best interests to do so. As we widen the pool of students who are both equal and excellent, colleges will be able to admit the most accomplished without regard to politically unpopular affirmative action prerequisites. More important, they will be able to admit students who already are capable of doing what colleges and universities are in business to teach young people to do: think for themselves. Duke's Christoph Guttentag says that in many ways, "A student's learning only begins when he gets to college." By starting that learning years earlier, colleges would be able to teach a great deal more than they do now, and students would enter the real world better prepared to cope with the information society of the twenty-first century.

□ □ □ ❚ □

In early June, Princeton University held commencement exercises for the two hundred and forty-sixth time.

At the first commencement in 1748, Princeton president and later U.S. vice president Aaron Burr spoke in Latin, from memory, for three-quarters of an hour. He was followed by the student salutatorian, who also spoke in Latin.

At the two hundred and forty-sixth, President Shapiro spoke in English. But the student salutatorian, following tradition, delivered his speech in Latin. His classmates, few of whom knew much Latin (certainly not as much as past generations of Princeton students were required to know), managed to cheer, laugh, and hiss in all the right places. But then, they had been provided with written instruction sheets.

As they have since 1922, weather permitting, the graduating students, their parents, and their invited guests gathered on the giant lawn in front of Nassau Hall. A number of honorary degrees were conferred upon, among others, a poet, an economist, a chemist, a playwright, a businessman, and a lawyer who works for children's rights—a mix that reinforced the message that the Pursuit of Happiness can go down many different roads. Two days before, another honorary degree had been conferred on a former Princeton professor of art and archeology; he had accepted his award from Shapiro in a hospital bed. He had died the next day, embraced to the last by the Princeton community.

In his commencement address, Shapiro said, "The idea of continuing to build a national culture that transcends individual cultures while somehow giving voice, place, honor, and value to our separate identities, histories, and traditions is audacious, complex, risky, and certainly daunting. It is a grand design—which we must continue to perfect—for the inclusion of others in a common dream that is part melting pot, part negotiated mosaic. My reading of American history highlights both the great strength we have gained by this approach of inclusiveness and the great distance we have yet to travel in order to more fully realize the benefits of this grand experiment. To participate in the ongoing construction and reconstruction of our open society is a task that is worthy of our greatest energies." The goal of everyone, Shapiro added, should be "to assume the role of citizen in ensuring that we create a society that lifts each of us to new levels of achievement, understanding, and humanity."

In his address, the class valedictorian said that "in order to start raising a generation of children who read books, we must first educate a generation of future parents who do not. My classmates, that is our generation. . . . Personally, I'm embarrassed to mention all the books I haven't read. Of course we can each fill in our personal gaps. We are educated enough to know what we ought to have read. But even if I never read Cervantes, I know I will be reading *Pat the Bunny* because I believe that the most important reading we will ever do isn't the last one hundred books or the next one hundred but the reading we will do for our children."

A FINAL THOUGHT

It really is impossible to craft a college application that makes the applicant into someone he or she is not. For all its flaws, the admissions process is nonetheless able to get beneath the glorified surfaces of young people—as represented by their grades and test scores—and reveal their inner nature. It's that inner nature, that capacity and potential for future learning and leadership, that elite colleges are hunting for. It can't be faked; it must be built up over time.

Although it might seem otherwise to a college-frantic high school senior, the *real* value of understanding the selective college admissions process lies in realizing the importance of being oneself, of following one's own muse, of doing things for the sheer joy of them—even within the seemingly goal-oriented world of education.

"Being yourself" may mean going in an unexpected direction—even discovering that your "self" doesn't really fit in with the academic intensity of a place like Princeton after all. The real point is not so much where you go to school as how you live your life. If you're learning, growing, and pursuing your own interests with a passion—I'd say you've already got the better part of the bargain.

BIBLIOGRAPHY

AMABILE, TERESA M. *Growing Up Creative.* New York: Crown, 1989. Good reading for parents interested in subtly trying to get their child to make the most of his or her creative talent.

BELL, TERRELL H. *Active Parent Concern.* Englewood Cliffs, NJ: Prentice-Hall, 1976. Dry reading, but good as a starting point for parents who want to improve their children's school and home education.

COOKSON, PETER W., JR., and CAROLINE HODGES PERSELL. *Preparing for Power: America's Elite Boarding Schools.* New York: Basic Books, 1985. Excellent analysis of the preppie culture in America and the advantages that money can buy.

CSIKSZENTMIHALYI, MIHALY, KEVIN RATHUNDE, and SAMUEL WHALEN. *Talented Teenagers: The Roots of Success and Failure.* Cambridge: Cambridge University Press, 1993. An analysis of very bright students reflecting on the social problems of "geeks" and "nerds."

DAY, DONALD, ed. *Woodrow Wilson's Own Story.* Boston: Little, Brown and Company, 1952. The chapter on "Education and Democracy" is a must. Points out the "modern" ideas of affirmative action were first espoused by Wilson nearly a century ago.

ELFIN, MEL, ed. *America's Best Colleges*. Washington, DC: U.S. News & World Report, 1994. The statistical bible of college admissions. Nobody does it better, but it should serve only as an indicator of the colleges a student is qualified to get into, not schools he or she will, or would want, to attend.

FISKE, EDWARD B. *Smart Schools, Smart Kids*. New York: Simon & Schuster, 1991. Lively narrative of the Sizer- and Gardner-inspired revolution. Shows how parents can bring the revolution to their children's schools.

GARDNER, HOWARD. *Frames of Mind: The Theory of Multiple Intelligences*. New York: Basic Books, 1983. One of the two books a parent should read before Sizer and Fiske. Spells out why high schools probably don't teach children the way they learn best.

GARDNER, HOWARD. *The Unschooled Mind: How Children Think and How Schools Should Teach*. New York: Basic Books, 1991. The other book a parent should read before Sizer and Fiske. Highlights schools where Gardner's thinking has taken root and inspires parents to make changes in their own children's schools.

GARDNER, JOHN W. *Excellence: Can We Be Equal and Excellent Too?* New York: Norton, 1984. A short, thoughtful essay not just on excellence but on quality, both personal and professional.

GEORGES, CHRISTOPHER J. *One Hundred Successful College Application Essays*. New York: NAL-Dutton, 1991. Read Hargadon's introduction.

KLITGAARD, ROBERT E. *Choosing Elites*. New York: Basic Books, 1985. An "inside the admissions office" look at the process, focusing heavily on Harvard.

LEITCH, ALEXANDER. *A Princeton Companion*. Princeton, NJ: Princeton University Press, 1978. An encyclopedia of facts about the university, best enjoyed by loyal alumni.

MACGOWAN, SANDRA F., and MCGINTY, SARAH M., eds. *50 College Admission Directors Speak to Parents*. Orlando, FL: Harcourt

Brace Jovanovich, 1988. Another "inside the admissions office" book, this one in admissions officers' own words. A broad overview, with short and general sections that may or may not answer a parent's or student's specific questions.

MATTHAY, EILEEN R., ed. *Counseling for College: A Professional's Guide to Motivating, Advising, and Preparing Students for Higher Education.* Princeton, NJ: Peterson's Guides, 1991. A useful book for all high school guidance counselors.

MCCLEERY, WILLIAM. *Conversations on the Character of Princeton.* Princeton, NJ: Princeton University Press, 1986. Obviously biased, this slim volume is still worth reading for the student interested in knowing whether Princeton would be a good match.

MULLIN, MARK H. *Educating for the 21st Century.* Lanhan, MD: Madison, 1991. Unusual perspective by an insightful educator. Not required reading, but thought-provoking and worth the time.

ORDOVENSKY, PAT, and ROBERT THORNTON. *Opening College Doors.* New York: HarperCollins, 1992. An excellent primer on the process. Most useful for its enactments of real admissions committee meetings.

PASCARELLA, ERNEST T., and PATRICK T. TERENZINI. *How College Affects Students.* San Francisco: Jossey-Bass, 1991. A book for educational, psychological, and sociological professionals, with a reassuring message for every student who doesn't get into an elite school.

PIERSON, GEORGE W. *The Education of American Leaders.* New York: Praeger, 1969. A fascinating antique, most useful today as an indicator of just how narrow the corridors of power in America once were.

RAVITCH, DIANE. *The Schools We Deserve.* New York: Praeger, 1985. A series of essays about the quality of education in America today that may anger you enough to storm the next board of education meeting.

Sizer, Theodore R. *Horace's School—Redesigning the American High School*. Boston: Houghton Mifflin, 1992. A must-read for parents, teachers, and school administrators. Spells out clearly both the theory and the procedures for reforming secondary education in a way that benefits the student.

Synott, Maria Graham. *The Half-Opened Door: Discrimination and Admissions at Harvard, Yale, and Princeton, 1900–1970*. Westport, CT: Greenwood Press, 1979. This one will surprise even old-timers who know firsthand that the elite colleges used to be bastions of privilege and prejudice. An interesting weave of prejudice on campus with prejudice in American society.

Wechsler, Harold S. *The Qualified Student: A History of Selective College Admission in America*. New York: Wiley, 1977. Not highly informative about college admissions today, but a surprisingly readable account of how college admissions developed in this country.

Wickenden Associates. *Your Guide to the College Admissions Process*. Princeton, NJ: Wickenden Associates, 1991. Excellent advice from a former admissions dean who has kept his hand in the business.

INDEX